D1164034

NON-FICTION

270.1 Sh3

Sheaffer, Robert

Making of the Messiah :Christianity
and resentment

9000705913

A

DO NOT REMOVE CARD FROM POCKET

Mead Public Library
Sheboygan, Wisconsin

Each borrower is held responsible for all library
materials drawn on his card and for all fines
accruing on same.

DEMCO

DISCARDED
Mead Public Library

The Making
of the Messiah

The Making of the Messiah

Christianity and Resentment

Robert Sheaffer

Prometheus Books
Buffalo, New York

Published 1991 by Prometheus Books

The Making of the Messiah: Christianity and Resentment. Copyright ©
1991 by Robert Sheaffer. All rights reserved. No part of this publication
may be reproduced, stored in a retrieval system, or transmitted in
any form or by any means, electronic, mechanical, photocopying,
recording, or otherwise, without prior written permission of the
publisher, except in the case of brief quotations embodied in critical
articles and reviews. Inquiries should be addressed to Prometheus
Books 700 East Amherst Street, Buffalo, New York 14215, 716-
837-2475. FAX: 716-835-6901.

95 94 93 92 91   5 4 3 2 1

Library of Congress Cataloging-in-Publication Data

Sheaffer, Robert.
    The Making of the Messiah : Christianity and Resentment /
by Robert Sheaffer.
        p.   cm.
    Includes bibliographical references and index.
    ISBN 0-87975-691-8 (hard : alk. paper)
    1. Christianity—Origin. I. Title.
BR129.S49   1991
270.1—dc.20   91-27091
                                                             CIP

Printed in the United States of America on acid-free paper.

705913

Dedicated to Celsus,
A Roman Philosopher About Whom Little is Known,
Yet Who Had the Keys to the Puzzle around the Year 170!

Contents

Introduction*

This book presents a picture of the origins of Christianity very different from anything that has been published before. Many Christians will find this book as offensive as Moslem fanatics did Salman Rushdie's "blasphemous" *Satanic Verses*. This book contains a reinterpretation of Christianity's beginnings, attempting to set aside myths about the life of Jesus that are unsupported by sound scholarship. Our purpose in writing is to make apparent why Christian Doctrines and Scriptures assumed their present form. All the sources cited in this work are publicly available, nearly all of them in English. Most of them have been available for decades, and some for centuries. None of them are unknown to biblical scholars, or even greatly unfamiliar. It is the way these sources are pieced together, and the picture that emerges from them, that will generate so much controversy.

The most immediate difficulty confronting any work on this subject is that biblical scholars, as we shall see in the pages that follow, do not agree even among themselves about many important facts. For example, most scholars agree that the Gospel of Matthew was

*I would like to thank Robert F. Suchor, Paul Kurtz, Fred Acquistapace, and Martin S. Kottmeyer for making many helpful suggestions. I would also like to thank Henry Palka and Robert Steiner for sending me valuable materials and information. Bible quotes are from the King James Version unless otherwise indicated.

written around the years 80–85. Yet at least one influential scholar insists that it was no later than 39 (see p. 96). Scholars generally accept that the books of the New Testament were composed in Greek as they now stand, and that Mark is the oldest of the three Synoptic Gospels. Yet you can find a few scholars with impressive credentials who will sharply disagree with those statements. All responsible biblical scholars acknowledge that several of the Epistles in the New Testament attributed to Paul were in fact written after Paul's death by someone else, but falsely attributed to Paul to bolster their authority. However, disagreement remains as to which Epistles were written by Paul, and which by impostors.

In light of problems such as these, be assured that you will undoubtedly be able to find statements emanating from the most credible of sources to contradict many statements you will read here. But you can also be assured that there is some credible source behind every factual claim, and that where my own opinion is offered, this will be clear to the reader. I accept the prevailing consensus on New Testament chronology and synoptic development almost without exception. What I have attempted to do is to formulate a "best fit" scenario for a rational, secular interpretation of the origin of Christianity, one accounting for the greatest possible number of presumed facts, while minimizing the variance with probable historical truth. That a particular hypothesis seems grossly shocking or abhorrent to a practicing Christian, or runs counter to popularly received accounts was not considered an argument against it. I realize that the scenario I depict will not be without some problems. But to maintain as historically accurate the traditional interpretation of Christianity— whether based on a literalistic interpetation of the Bible or on conventional scholarship—results in problems greater still.

Much of what this book has to say is not merely impious or heretical, but literally blasphemous, and to an extreme degree. I do not shock the reader for the mere pleasure of doing so. Instead, I present what I believe to be historical truth. These truths are highly disagreeable to the Christian religion, having been kept from the public eye by centuries of church censorship and blasphemy laws. Even the great unbelievers of centuries past stepped right up to the boundary that I cross, but turned back at the last possible moment, censoring themselves out of fear of the consequences. In *The Decline and Fall of the Roman Empire*, Gibbon cited and translated a highly inflammatory passage from the Church Father Tertullian, but stopped short at the very point where a blasphemous and major anti-Christian charge was about to be addressed. Gibbon wryly remarked that "the humanity of the reader will permit me to draw a veil over the rest of this infernal description." Nietzsche placed this same passage from Tertullian in its entirety in his *Genealogy of Morals*, but only in the original Latin, although he allowed himself the luxury of making a snide remark in German at the point where Gibbon stopped translating.

Voltaire, in his *Philosophical Dictionary*, went even so far as to mention the highly blasphemous ancient Jewish text, the *Toldoth Jeshu*, which deals with the matter from which Gibbon and Nietzsche shied away, although Voltaire does not explain to the curious reader what the book is, or where it comes from. He titillates us with a little of what it says, but is careful not to say too much. He pretends to be horrified by it, but the intelligent reader is not fooled.

Voltaire was wise to be so cautious. Soon after his *Philosophical Dictionary* was published in the summer of 1765, three young men in Abbeville, France, were accused of defiling a crucifix, showing disrespect to a religious procession, and singing obscene and blasphemous songs about the Virgin Mary, whose lyrics those passages of Voltaire might well have inspired. One of the three young men wisely fled before he could be apprehended, but another turned "state's evidence" against the other two. Monsieur d'Etallonde, who had fled, was sentenced *in absentia* to do penance while wearing around his neck the inscription "Damned and Despised Blasphemer." He was then to have his tongue torn out, his hand cut off, and to be burned alive. Fortunately for d'Etallonde, the worst the judges could do was threaten this of his effigy.

But the nineteen-year-old Jean François Lefevbre, Chevalier de la Barre, was not so fortunate. He was sentenced to undergo torture, both in the ordinary and the extraordinary degree, which was intended to wring from him a confession of his horrid blasphemy. He was then to do penance in public, before having his tongue torn out and then being beheaded. This resolute young man endured the torture, even in the extraordinary degree, yet still refused to confess to the charges before him. He likewise adamantly refused to perform the public penance. He so desperately resisted the executioners' attempts to tear out his tongue that they satisfied themselves with a pretense of having done so. He bravely submitted his neck to the sword, and afterward both body and head were burned, along with a copy of Voltaire's *Philosophical Dictionary*, the book blamed for leading these men astray. Voltaire was outraged at such barbarism, and spent the rest of his life battling *l'infâme*, which to him meant one thing: Christianity.

Likewise the Jews, custodians of much invaluable information about the early years of Christianity, have been censored, or have even censored themselves, in order better to enjoy peace with their more numerous, and often highly intolerant, Christian neighbors. The *Encyclopaedia Judaica Jerusalem* states: "Beginning with the Basle edition of the Talmud (1578-1580), those passages in which Jesus was mentioned, as well as other statements alluding to Christianity, were deleted from most editions of the Babylonian Talmud by the Christian censors or even by internal Jewish censorship." Jews who refused to cooperate had their sacred writings seized and burned. Literally thousands of scrolls were consigned to the flames. The pretext for this outrage was that the offending passages "blasphemed" Jesus and his mother.[1] These censored passages paint a very different picture of the life of Jesus than we read in the gospels. Fortunately, the scholarship of the past century has recovered the majority of what was lost. It is on these censored passages that much of this book's thesis rests.

Yet the Jews' self-censorship has still not ended. The validity and relevance of those passages most damaging to Christianity are sometimes disputed by contemporary Jewish scholars, even though their validity has been accepted by other scholars with little or no reservation. The reason why these scholars downplay the validity of records that they themselves perhaps believe to be historically correct, is probably a fear of increased anti-Semitism. Nonetheless, sooner or later a time must come when such matters can be freely read and discussed by rational adults, and the facts decided on their own merit. That time is now.

In our own century, blasphemy laws hinder the publication of a work such as this. Blasphemy laws are still on the books in Britain, even if not always strictly enforced, and it is likely that any British edition of this book would get its publisher in trouble with the law. Indeed, one Member of Parliament who has a large Moslem population in his district recently introduced a bill to extend those blasphemy laws to punish not only insults to Christianity, but to Islam as well.[2] In Italy today, blasphemy laws still forbid defaming what is deemed holy by the Roman Catholic Church, and a recent formal decree of the Italian Constitutional Court recommended that these statutes against blasphemy not merely be maintained, but extended to cover other religious denominations as well.[3]

Even in the United States, freedom of speech on such matters is by no means assured. The State of Massachusetts, which fancies itself a haven for institutions of higher learning, still carries on its books a law against any speech that "willfully blasphemes" the "holy name of God." Even as this page is being written, a tape of a speech given at Harvard University by a Boston-area secular humanist is being scrutinized by state prosecutors with a view toward prosecuting the speaker for blasphemy.[4] Any Massachusetts professor who reads this book aloud in class runs the risk of criminal prosecution, should some Christian student seek to press charges.

This combination of censorship and persecution has succeeded in keeping many of the facts herein contained practically unknown, except to a small number of scholars. Most of these scholars are themselves churchmen, dedicated to combatting blasphemy, not to studying it. In at least one recent scholarly work, the above-mentioned passage of Tertullian would seem to have been deliberately mistranslated, apparently to hide blasphemous statements about Jesus' mother. My discussions with numerous highly educated secular humanists and atheists have thus far not turned up a single individual who is aware of the principal facts this book contains, no matter how much of the literature of unbelief they may have read. Similarly, most educated Jews are unaware even of the existence of the Toldoth.

Fortunately, Christian fundamentalists are more civilized than their Moslem counterparts; it has been two centuries since the Church attempted to suppress heresy by murdering the heretic. But more subtle methods of attempting to silence dissent yet remain. The existence of this book is a triumph of the First Amendment. Only where the freedom of speech is vigorously defended as an absolute can a book like this be published, sold, and openly read and discussed. There are no doubt countries that will not knowingly allow this book to cross their border. There will probably be many groups in the United States that will attempt to keep it out of bookstores. Some parents and educators will undoubtedly try to have it pulled off library shelves, and fundamentalists will seek to have it boycotted, suppressed, or worse. But as long as this book remains freely available to all who seek it, readers will know that their own freedom of speech remains inviolate.

NOTES

1. *Encyclopaedia Judaica Jerusalem* (1971 ed.), s.v. "Jesus." See also "Talmud, Burning of.".

2. Daniel Pipes, "Pluralism in Peril," *Reason* (July 1989): 42.

3. Roberto La Ferla, "The Vatican's Pact with Italy," *Free Inquiry* 11, no. 1 (Winter 1990–91): 36.

4. Free Inquiry, *Secular Humanist Bulletin* (February 1990).

1

Immaculate Fornication?

*"For the love of this world is fornication
against thee."*
St. Augustine, Confessions 1:13

While tens of millions of Bible-believing Christians unceasingly assert
that the New Testament is the "revealed word of God," the problem
of its origin is not nearly as simple as they make it out to be. Every
educated person who is willing to be the least bit honest on the subject
has to admit that the gospels, in their present form, were written
at least a generation after the death of Jesus, and have experienced
some modification in the years that followed. The New Testament
books were not all written at the same time, or in the same place,
and there are many unanswered questions concerning their date, content, and authorship. Some of the books have variant texts in different
manuscripts, raising the question of which version is genuinely "inspired." Biblical scholars continued to debate when the four Gospels, and indeed the entire New Testament, were composed. We have,
for example, most of a gospel attributed to Peter, which was used
in worship by early Christians about the year 150 A.D. That it is
not part of the Bible today is the consequence of arbitrary decisions.

The New Testament as we know it today was fixed in content
in the year 367 A.D. by the Festal Epistle of St. Athanasius, Archbishop

of Alexandria, more than three centuries after the death of Jesus. At the same time he sent out a solemn order to purge all "apocryphal" or "heretical" books, meaning that all Christian writings not included in this Canon of the New Testament were to be burned. In 1945, a major discovery was made near Nag Hammadi, Egypt, of long-lost gospels and other texts that were used in worship by the "heretical" Gnostic sect. These texts had apparently been hidden by some dissident to escape the wrath of Athanasius,[1] since the Gnostic church was forcibly suppressed by the stronger Catholic faction. Unless we assume that "might makes right" in the determination of religious questions, there is no *a priori* reason for saying that Gnostic writings should be any more or less credible than those of Orthodoxy. No matter what the fundamentalists may tell us, the New Testament is not a single book, written by a human scribe taking Divine dictation, but an arbitrary compendium of ancient texts that are claimed to have been divinely inspired. However, what makes one such book divine truth, and another "apocryphal," or even "heretical," is not readily discerned.

THE *TOLDOTH JESHU*

There exists a remarkable and enigmatic book of great antiquity, written in Hebrew, called *Toldoth Jeshu*: "The Generations of Jesus." Its antiquity is not seriously in question. Hugh J. Schonfield, a well-known writer on early Christianity, judges the main portion of the book to be a fourth-century work. The biblical scholar R. Joseph Hoffmann judges it to be fifth century.[2]

But the Toldoth clearly draws upon material that is far older still. Voltaire mentions this work both in his *Philosophical Dictionary*,[3] and in his *Letter Concerning the Jews*. Voltaire says that the second-century Roman writer Celsus cites the Toldoth "with confidence." This is not correct. While Celsus' arguments against Christianity parallel those in the Toldoth—Celsus states that he is telling us facts that are known among the Jews—we do not know whether Celsus actually read that work, or possibly a predecessor to it, since none of the works of Celsus have survived (except what is quoted by Origen, attempting to refute him), undoubtedly because they were "heretical" in the extreme. What we *can* say with confidence is that much of the material now in the Toldoth was known to Celsus around the year 170. Clearly, the Toldoth is no "Medieval Jewish forgery," as many pious Christian apologists would like us to believe (as well as some Jews who are fearful of renewed anti-Semitism).

Celsus charged that at his time the Christians had already "corrupted the Gospel from its original integrity, to a threefold, and fourfold, and manifold degree, and have remodeled it, so that they might be able to answer objections." We do know that Origen, the third-century Church Father who mutilated himself in the pursuit of holy chastity, sets out to refute Celsus by arguing as if he were addressing the main points of the Toldoth itself.[4] Origen apparently felt that the only way he could avoid those "sins of the flesh" that imperiled his salvation was to cut off the very flesh making such transgression possible. This does not exactly suggest that the blessed Father possessed any of the iron self-control that was so admired and prized among the noble Romans; it suggests instead he must have been viewed by them as something irresolute and pathetic. Commenting on the familiar injunction, "if thine eye offend thee, pluck it out" (Mark 9:47), Nietzsche wryly remarks, "It is not precisely the eye that is meant."[5]

Thus the Toldoth, like many other existing religious texts, is clearly drawn from sources much older still, sources which no longer survive. Furthermore, as Schonfield illustrates, it seems to draw upon very ancient Christian writings that have since vanished; he notes many parallels in the Toldoth with those few fragments preserved of the long-lost Hebrew-language gospel, whose author is reputed to have been the apostle Matthew. It likewise has many parallels, both in language and content, with the four canonical Gospels, most clearly with Mark. Schonfield notes that "it is as if we had reflected in the Toldoth a fifth gospel, by means of which we could further investigate the other four";[6] he believes that the reflection seen is that of the now vanished Hebrew gospel.

The three Gospels of Matthew, Mark, and Luke are known to scholars as the "Synoptic Gospels," because they have many passages which are nearly identical, and tell essentially the same story in the same sequence. They are obviously related textually to each other. Mark is undoubtedly the oldest of the three; Matthew was written next, then Luke. The fourth canonical Gospel, that attributed to John, is significantly different in content and approach from the other three. Schonfield notes that it is remarkable how the author of the Toldoth has been able to "delve so deeply into the Synoptic Problem, and discover the connection between divergent stories in the Synoptics and John."[7]

This would indicate that the Toldoth, far from being a late forgery as some have charged, is very ancient, indeed so ancient that it draws from long-vanished sources that are at least as fundamental as Mark and John.

The Hebrews, and other ancient peoples, had a custom of naming a book by its first words; for example, Exodus is known in Hebrew as "Shemoth," from its opening words "we-eleh shemoth." The title *Toldoth Jeshu* indicates a derivation from (or at least an obvious allusion to) some work beginning with those words. The canonical Gospel of Matthew opens with the words, "The book of the Generation of Jesus." If that Gospel was originally written in Hebrew (as a few scholars maintain), the Hebrew version of Matthew would have been known as the *Toldoth Jeshu*.[8] Hence Schonfield suggests that the Toldoth may represent a nearly pristine form of the now lost Hebrew gospel attributed to Matthew, which I consider most unlikely; its author's viewpoint is obviously not that of a Christian. However, the Toldoth may well contain some material in common with that lost work.

Some of the details of Jesus' life in the *Memoirs of the Apostles* of St. Justin Martyr, written about the year 150, are closer to the Toldoth than they are to any of the four canonical Gospels.[9] It is entirely possible (although by no means certain) that in the *Toldoth Jeshu*, reflecting information that has been in rabbinical hands since the earliest days of Christianity, we may have preserved for our inspection a gospel that was *not* altered by the kind of doctoring by Christian evangelists to which Celsus bitterly refers. The Toldoth may well be the closest thing to the original accounts of the life of Jesus that is still in existence.

What does this bold and enigmatic document have to say? While on some points it does confirm orthodoxy and the writings of Church Fathers, it has (from the Christian standpoint) the audacity to challenge the interpretation of virtually all major points of dogma. Furthermore, it does so in a way that not only allows us to trace the process of pious doctoring taking place, *but it allows us to see that the doctoring was done in a manner to exacerbate proletarian resentments against the Roman authorities*. The summary below is drawn primarily from the nearly complete translation of the Toldoth by Hugh J. Schonfield in his book *According to the Hebrews*; any reader wishing to pursue this matter further must necessarily begin there. Here, then, is the story told in the *Toldoth Jeshu*:

Chapter 1:

Jesus' mother, Mary, was the daughter of Hannah of the land of Galilee. She was betrothed to John (not Joseph!), a descendant of King David, who was learned and godly.

But at the door of her house came a man, a handsome warrior, named Pandera (spelled variously as Pantera or Panthera): he "cast his eyes upon her." (At this point Schonfield omits seven verses out of sensitivity to his Christian readers. These verses describe the seduction of Mary by Pandera, she believing that this man was her betrothed.)

When John arrived, and heard this, he realized that Pandera had "done this deed," and he left Mary. He consulted the Rabbi Simeon, the son of Shetach. (Here Schonfield omits another verse that repeats the seduction story.) The rabbi asks him who has done this, and John replies, "the son of Pandera, for he is nigh unto her house, and a seeker after fornication." The rabbi advises John that if there were no witnesses to this event, he should keep silent. The seducer will probably return a second time, and this time he must arrange for there to be witnesses.

After some time had passed, it was widely noted that Mary was pregnant. But John, her betrothed, protested, "Not by me is she with child." Being unwilling to stay and hear himself reproached for this dishonor, he went away to Babylon, and never returned.

Later, Mary bore a son, who was named Jesus after his mother's brother, "but after his despicableness was revealed they called him Jesu" (Esau?)

(Apparently several years pass.) Jesus' mother "brought him before a teacher" to learn the Halacha and the Talmud.

(Here apparently a good many more years pass.) It was demanded by tradition that no young man should enter the synagogue without covering his head and lowering his eyes, out of respect for the masters. But one day "that wicked one" came by while the rabbis were studying scripture, and he refused to salute them, or bow, or cover his head. One of the rabbis said, "he is a bastard." Another added that he was indeed illegitimate, the son of a woman "in her separation."

On another day, the rabbis were debating the civil code of the Talmud, and Jesus came and began to "utter halacoth" (theological law) to them. One of them asked Jesus if he was aware that anyone who says a "halacha" in the presence of his master is worthy of death. Jesus suggests that it is he who is the master, and compares himself to Moses and Jethro. When the elders heard this, they said, "since he is so very shameless," let us find out more about him. They sent for his mother, and asked her who is the father of that child. Mary replied that he is the son of her husband John, who has left her and gone away to Babylon. But Rabbi Simeon, the son of Shetach, was there, and he replied that thirty years earlier John, her betrothed, had come to him, and had revealed what had happened. John "for great shame" had left her and gone to Babylon, never to return. There is, however, no judgment of death upon Mary for her adultery, since she did it "not wittingly; but Joseph the son of Pandera sought occasion for fornication every day." When Mary heard Rabbi Simeon say that there was no judgment of death against her, she admitted the truth of what he had said. But when this account became widely known, the people said of Jesus, "he is a bastard and the son of a woman in her separation and worthy of death." Jesus then fled to Jerusalem.

Chapter 2:

Israel was ruled by a woman named Helene. (This is not historical.) In the temple was a holy stone, and on it were engraved the letters of the "Ineffable Name." (The "Ineffable Name" is "YAHWEH," the name of the all-powerful deity, whose name orthodox Jews consider it blasphemous to say, or even write.) Someone who learned this name could do anything he wanted. However, to keep this name secret, two dogs of brass were tied to pillars at the door of the temple, and as someone exited the temple, these dogs would bray at him, which erased the letters from his mind. But Jesus came and learned those letters, and wrote them on parchment. He painlessly cut open the flesh of his thigh, and put the parchment inside, then restored his flesh. As he exited, the dogs bayed at him, causing him to forget the letters.

But on arriving home, Jesus cut into his thigh once again, extracted the parchment, and memorized the letters. He then went outside, and gathered a crowd of three hundred and ten young men. "People call me a bastard," said Jesus, "yet I am the son of a virgin." He cites the scriptural prophecies of the Messiah, including that of a virgin birth (a claim based upon a mistranslation of "young woman" as "virgin"). The crowd asks to see proof of his claims. They bring him a lame man. Jesus said the letters of the Name over him, and the man rose to his feet. The crowd then worshiped him and hailed him as the Messiah. Jesus next cured a leper in the same way. All the "insurgents" of the people joined him, "the wicked of Israel, brigands and transgressors."

Chapter 3:

When the "wise men" saw how many people believed in Jesus, they seized him and brought him before Helene, the queen, saying, "this man is a sorcerer, who deceives the people." Jesus replied that the Scriptures foretold of his coming. The queen asked them whether this was true. They replied that such was the prophecy, but it did not describe Jesus, for "with this bastard the signs are not present." Jesus reaffirmed that he was the Messiah, and claimed to be able to revive the dead. She ordered to have brought the body of someone who had recently died. Jesus "spake the letters" and the body revived. The queen trembled, and was very impressed. She dismissed the disgraced elders.

The "insurgents and wrongdoers of Israel" followed Jesus in evergreater numbers. Jesus went to Upper Galilee. The elders returned to the queen, and once again accused Jesus of sorcery, and of leading the people astray. She sent out horsemen after Jesus. They found him once again before a crowd, claiming to be the son of God. The horsemen attempted to arrest him, but the people fought on his behalf. Jesus told them not to fight, but to trust in the power of God. The people were making birds of clay; Jesus spoke the "Ineffable Name," and they came alive and flew off. Within an hour, these birds fell back to the ground. Jesus told the people to bring him a millstone, which they rolled to the sea; he again spoke the letters, and made it to float on the water while he sat on it. Jesus then told the horsemen to return to the queen, and tell her what they had seen. Then "the spirit" lifted him up from the waters to the land.

When the horsemen related this to the queen, she trembled once again. She once more sent for the elders, and for Jesus as well. The elders took one Judas Iscariot, and brought him into the Temple's "holy of holies." Judas wrote the letters on parchment, cut painlessly into his thigh, and hid the parchment therein, just as Jesus had done. When Jesus arrived before the queen, he once again cited prophecy, claiming that heaven would receive him, and he lifted his arms and flew like an eagle. However, Judas Iscariot spoke these same letters, and flew in the same way. Judas attempted to bring Jesus down to earth, but was unable to do so because both of them possessed the "Ineffable Name." Judas then "befouled" Jesus, polluting him and causing both of them to fall to the earth. This somehow negated the power of the "Ineffable Name," allowing the queen's men to seize Jesus.

They covered Jesus' head, and "smote him with pomegranate staves." Jesus then called to his followers to rise up for him. He was taken to the Synagogue of Tiberias, and bound to a pillar. There was much fighting between the "fools and impious ones" who believed Jesus, and the supporters of the queen. Jesus cited prophecy once again, was given vinegar to drink, and was crowned with thorns. The fighting continued. Jesus recited more prophecies, and his supporters began to stone the officials. Jesus' three hundred and ten disciples enabled him to escape, and brought him to Antioch, where he stayed until the eve of the Passover.

Chapter 4:

The Passover that year fell on a Sabbath day. Jesus came into Jerusalem on the eve of the Passover with his disciples, riding on an ass, reciting more prophecies. He entered the Temple with his three hundred and ten disciples. One of those disciples (some texts call him "Judas," others "a thief") went to the "wise men," and offered to identify Jesus to them if he was paid; the disciples had sworn not to tell who was their leader. (Another variant text of the Toldoth has a similar situation and passage in chapter 3, in which Judas says, "that man before whom I bow down and prostrate myself, that is the bastard.")

The disciples in the temple with Jesus greeted those other disciples who had gathered to pray on the Mount of Olives on the Passover. Judas (or "the thief") bowed to "the wicked Jesus," who was immediately arrested. The elders questioned Jesus; he again replied by citing prophecies. Jesus was held securely, and his followers were unable to help him escape. When Jesus saw that he was going to die, he cited prophecies of how God's prophet woul be slain by the sword.

Jesus was put to death (one manuscript says he was taken "to the place of stoning"), in the sixth hour of the eve of the Passover and Sabbath. They then attempted to hang his body on a tree, but the tree limb broke. It was deduced that Jesus had known that it was the "custom of Israel" to hang the body of an executed person on a tree, and had used the "Ineffable Name" so that no tree would bear him. However, the carob stock is not a tree but "a plant" (it is actually an evergreen tree with edible seed pods), and hence the spell had no effect. Jesus' body was hung on the carob tree until the time of afternoon prayer. They then took him down and buried him. (Deuteronomy 21:23 commands that executed persons hanged on a tree must be taken down and buried before sundown, or else the land given thee by "the LORD thy God" would be "defiled.")

Chapter 5:

On the day after the Sabbath, "the insurgents" were weeping by Jesus' grave. (On the Sabbath day, of course, virtually no normal activities were permitted; this was thus the disciples' first opportunity to visit the grave of their slain leader.) Some young men came by, and after insulting those followers of Jesus, asked them why they were weeping. Apparently Jesus' body was no longer in its grave. "The insurgents" went to Queen Helene, proclaiming that the one who had been slain must surely have been the Messiah, for he worked wonders, and now his body was no longer in its grave. He must already have ascended into heaven, they said, in fulfillment of the prophecy (Psalms 49:15). The queen called in the elders, who reaffirmed that Jesus must be in his grave. However, a search of the area failed to turn up the body. Here the narrator states what none of these people knew at the time: that the gardener had taken Jesus' body out of its grave, and buried it under an irrigation canal, whose water had been temporarily diverted. The queen became extremely angry, and threatened that unless they found the body of Jesus, they would be imprisoned. They asked for time to find it (one variant of the text says three days). The "insurgents" bewailed that the others had slain "the Lord's anointed."

All Israel was "in great distress." One of the elders, named Rabbi Tanchuma, was weeping as he walked in the field. When the gardener asks him why he is weeping, the rabbi replies that it is because of "that wicked one" who cannot be found. The time allotted by the queen is nearly up, and they have all been weeping and fasting. When the gardener heard about the general mourning, and the stories that Jesus had ascended into heaven, he replied that this shall be a day of gladness in Israel, for he had himself taken the body away so that "the insurgents" should not have it. Immediately the elders returned to Jerusalem with the glad tidings. A large crowd of people went back to the garden, and the body of Jesus was recovered. The body was dragged behind a horse through the streets of Jerusalem, and presented to the queen, who proclaimed that here was the one who was supposed to have ascended to heaven. The queen mocked "the insurgents" and praised the "wise men."

Chapter 6: The Acts of the Apostles

The disciples of Jesus dispersed to Mount Ararat, to Armenia, to Rome, and other places, causing the people there "to err." However, no matter where they went, the (Jewish) Lord caused these (Christian) disciples to be slain. Many of "the insurgents" in Israel "went astray" by following Jesus, causing great strife and destruction. "The insurgents" always rebuked the orthodox by charging that they had slain "the Lord's anointed." The orthodox countered by claiming that these others had followed a false prophet. This strife continued even thirty years after "that wicked one" had been slain. The elders concluded that Israel was being punished in this manner for its iniquities.

Thirty years after the death of Jesus, the elders asked one Elijah, a learned man, to go out into the desert to defeat and destroy the insurgents (in some manuscripts, he is known by other names). Elijah went to Antioch, and called upon all followers of Jesus to join him. Knowing the "Ineffable Name," Elijah heals the sick and the lame. Elijah proclaims himself to be the apostle of Jesus, and gains a large following. He tells them to "profane" the Sabbath, and keep the first day of the week holy instead. Instead of Passover, they are to celebrate the Resurrection. Instead of observing Jewish holidays such as the Day of Atonement, they are to observe the Christian holidays in their place. (The author of the Toldoth appears to be quite confused about what those Christian holidays are.) Circumcision is said to be no longer required. Elijah preached to them the sayings of Jesus, and thereby "separated" these people from Israel. This was done "for the restoration" of Israel; the "impious ones" were no longer Jews, and the strife ceased. The Nazarenes called this man "Paul." (This is the end of the Toldoth in some manuscripts.)

Chapter 7:

(Schonfield notes that chapters 7 and 8 are undoubtedly late additions to the book, as they describe events of the fifth century.) Nestorius, coming out of Persia, preaches a doctrine that stirs up strife among the Nazarenes. (The "Nestorian Heresy" was a fifth-century doctrine preached by the Patriarch of Constantinople, affirming that Christ had two separate natures, one human and one divine.)

Chapter 8:

Rabbi Simeon Kepha, the chief of the Sanhedrin, hears a voice from heaven. He climbs upon a high tower, and spends the rest of his life upon it. (This is obviously an account derived from the life of St. Simeon Stylites, who became a great celebrity in Christendom by proclaiming that the true holiness consisted of spending one's life sitting on a small platform atop a pillar. He spent thirty-five years up there, until his death in 459.)

Thus ends the intriguing and enigmatic tale told by the *Toldoth Jeshu.* Granting that this work, in its present form, dates from roughly the time that the canonical New Testament was assembled, and clearly reflects information a good deal older still, how seriously should it be taken? Is this merely a polemical and blasphemous account of the life of Jesus, fabricated by the Jews out of their dislike for the new, and to them heretical, sect? Or might it be a document reflecting now lost knowledge and writings, and perhaps the most historically accurate account of the story of Jesus still to survive?

JESUS, THE SON OF A VIRGIN?

We know from Matthew 1:18-20 that Joseph doubted the fidelity of his betrothed, a potentially embarrassing fact which no other Gospel admits, although this is abundantly clear in the Toldoth, as well as in various noncanonical Christian texts. However, in a convenient *deus ex machina*, Matthew wheels in an angel in Matt. 1:20-25, to tell Joseph that it is all right to proceed with the wedding, since Mary is still a virgin. It may be assumed, then, that this strained passage is intended to squelch less respectable accounts of Jesus' origin, such as that found in the Toldoth.

The Gospel of Matthew parallels the account of Mark quite closely on most matters. Jesus gives many of the same speeches, and works many of the same alleged miracles. We can line up many passages in Mark and Matthew (for example, Matt. 3:1 et. seq. with Mark 1:4, Matt. 21:1 with Mark 11:1, etc.), even though the passages themselves are not identical. Clearly, these two gospels, as well as Luke, are related. This is why Matthew, Mark, and Luke are known as the "Synoptic" Gospels. New Testament scholars generally agree that Matthew and Luke are derived from Mark. However, there is one major difference between Matthew and Mark. Mark gives no account whatsoever of Jesus' birth; Jesus simply appears on the scene. If we were to delete from Matthew verses 1:2 through the end of chapter 2—the portion recounting the strange genealogy of Jesus through Joseph, then telling his mother was a virgin—the beginning of Matthew would then look almost exactly like the beginning of Mark. Since Mark is, on the best evidence, the earlier work, this should alert us to the possibility that the account of Jesus' birth was *invented by the author of Matthew*, almost certainly to counter Jewish claims of the illegitimacy of Jesus' birth.

How all Jesus' siblings (see Mark 6:3) could have been born to a woman who is "perpetually virginal"—a doctrine accepted by Roman Catholics, the Eastern Orthodox, and Anglicans—is yet another example of a mystery too deep to be fathomed by mere human intellect. It is also to be wondered how believers in Mary's abhorrence of sex can reconcile this with Matthew 1:25, which states that Joseph "knew her not till she had brought forth her firstborn son," implying that the duration of her virginity was somewhat less than perpetual. Here we see how the Christian religion's hostility toward sex makes certain of its sects proclaim this mother of several children a "perpetual virgin," in direct contradiction of several verses of its own "sacred" texts!

The problem of Jesus' less-than-immaculate birth also surfaces in the Gospel of John, which is quite different in content from the three Synoptic Gospels. John, like Mark, gives no explanation whatsoever of Jesus' earthly origins, apart from the vague suggestion that "the Word was made flesh." This is presumably intended to convince the listener that words from heaven directly shaped and formed a human body, without the need of an earthly mother or father, thereby nicely bypassing the sticky problem of a woman whose pregnancy is disavowed by the man to whom she is betrothed.

A careful reading of the pseudo-Pauline epistle to Titus shows its author likewise quite sensitive to questions about Jesus' birth. (Nearly all scholars doubt that this letter was actually written by Paul, believing it to have been composed decades after Paul's death, about the same time as the Gospel of John.) "For there are many unruly and vain talkers and deceivers, especially they of the circumcision: whose mouths must be stopped, who subvert whole houses, teaching things which they ought not, for filthy lucre's sake. . . . Avoid foolish questions, and genealogies" (Titus 1:10–11, 3:9).

Reading between the lines, the problem apparently was that Christian evangelists would travel to some town, and make converts among the Gentiles. The Jews—"they of the circumcision"—finding people worshiping Jesus, would tell them about the illegitimate birth of their reputed Messiah. This would then "subvert whole houses" of Christians, undoing all the work of the disciples, and making the new religion a laughing stock. "Beware of Jews bearing genealogies" seems to be the message of this short letter. Remember that news traveled very slowly in those days, and could spread only by word of mouth. There were no newspapers or printed books, only laboriously handwritten scrolls. When a person who had never heard of this new religion was told by an evangelist that Jesus was a miracle worker and a Messiah, then heard someone else claim that Jesus was an unruly illegitimate son, there was no easy way for the listener to determine which of the two accounts was the more reliable except to gauge the credibility of the speaker. This explains the constant insistence throughout the Epistles that it is *our* accounts alone that constitute God's truth, and that all others are lying and blasphemous.

The Toldoth is not the only ancient work to assert the illegitimacy of Jesus' birth. There is a passage in the Talmud in which Rabbi Shimeon ben Azzai, who lived around the year 100, relates finding a genealogical scroll in Jerusalem on which was written "So-and-So, bastard son of an adulteress." Most scholars accept that the copious references to "so-and-so" or "that man" in the ancient Jewish writings refer in fact to Jesus of Nazareth; presumably Jesus' actions so infuriated the Jewish authorities that it pained them even to write or speak his name, much the way people today refer to one who continually brews trouble as "you know who." (Jews, as well as other ancient peoples, believed a name to have great power; merely to utter it might have unforeseen consequences.) During the Middle Ages, the Christians burned thousands of manuscripts of the Talmud, knowing that it contained passages such as this.[10]

CONFLICTING ACCOUNTS OF JESUS' DEATH AND RESURRECTION

Another significant and startling departure from orthodoxy in the Toldoth is that the cross plays no role whatsoever in the story of Jesus. Jesus is stoned to death by the Jews, and his body is afterward hung in a tree. One would expect that texts written by the ancient Jews themselves would seek to blame Jesus' execution upon the Romans, but in fact precisely the opposite is true: *all* the ancient Jewish writings are consistent in viewing the execution of Jesus as a purely internal matter involving only Jews. Before we dismiss this remarkable innovation as proof of the unreliability of its source, let us closely read the canonical Acts of the Apostles, which actually *confirms* the Toldoth's account of Jesus' death in three different passages! In Acts 5:30, Peter says not to the Romans, but to the Sanhedrin, the Jewish council of law, "The God of our fathers raised up Jesus, whom ye slew and hanged on a tree." In Acts 10:39, Peter once again speaks of Jesus, "whom they slew and hanged on a tree." And in Acts 13:28, Paul says "And when they had fulfilled all that was written of him, they took him down from the tree and laid him in a sepulchre." Jesus is also "hanged in a tree" in 1 Peter 2:24 and Galatians 3:13. *Thus, the account of Jesus' death given in five separate canonical verses agrees with the Toldoth, while differing with all four Gospels!* Christian apologists have offered the weak explanation that "the tree" is a metaphor representing "the cross." But note that Acts plainly states twice, and suggests a third time, that *Jesus was already dead by the time he was hung on the tree,* exactly as is written in the Toldoth. Far from casting suspicion on the Toldoth, the Acts of the Apostles, argued by some scholars to be among the oldest (and hence presumably least unreliable) books of the New Testament, enhances its credibility at this crucial point.

Peter, who claims to have actually witnessed "the sufferings of Christ" (1 Peter 5:1), tells us in his own epistle that Jesus ended up not on a cross, but on a tree: "Who with his own self bare our sins in his own body on the tree, that we, being dead to sins, would live unto righteousness" (1 Peter 2:24). And Paul tells us in Galatians 3:13: "Christ hath redeemed us from the curse of the [Mosaic] law, being made a curse for us: for it is written, cursed is every one that hangeth on a tree." The crucifixion account would thus seem to be a later "improvement" to the story of Jesus, one that was discovered to be far more effective in stirring up the resentments of "the insurgents" among the Gentiles.

Nor are these the only confirmations of the Toldoth's account of Jesus' death. There is a passage in the Talmud which says, "Tradition has it: On the eve (of the Sabbath and) of the Passover they hanged Jesus (the Nazarene)." And in the "heretical" Gnostic work, The Acts of John, we read: "He was hung on the tree of the cross. . . . Thou hearest that I suffered; yet I did not suffer: that I suffered not; yet I did suffer: that I was pierced; yet I was not smitten: that I was hanged; yet I was not hanged; that blood flowed from me; yet it did not flow."[11] In this confused passage, we see both the "hanging" and "crucifixion" versions related, although "hanging" predominates.

The Toldoth account of the Resurrection is, like the other major elements it contains of the life of Jesus, not only surprising and "heretical," but also much less favorable to the Christian interpretation. It is also less of an insult to common sense, and hence far more credible owing to its parsimony. The "evidence" for the Resurrection is that the body is missing, and nothing more. A short time later, perhaps a few days, the body is found, and the mystery is no more. As might be expected, however, a few days is enough time for the news of this incredible event to travel far and wide. When it is later related that Jesus' body was discovered and reburied, the listener faces a dilemma: which account is to be believed? In the absence of newspapers, photographs, and printed books, it is easy to see how a rumor of cosmic significance begun in such a dramatic manner might literally *never* die out.

The canonical Gospels tell the Resurrection story very differently—at least they do now. But the oldest existing copies of the Gospel of Mark, the father of the other two Synoptic Gospels, *ends with the discovery of the empty tomb.* Mark originally ended with what is now verse 16:8, on the words "for they were afraid"; the remaining twelve verses were added later![12]

Nobody claimed actually to have seen the risen Christ: that was added afterward. Thus the earliest Gospel account of the Resurrection is entirely consistent with what the Toldoth tells us; Jesus' body was somehow moved, and when his disciples discovered this fact, they were amazed and frightened. Nothing more was known of Jesus after this point. The following verses, in which the risen Jesus appears to his disciples, were added later, undoubtedly to answer charges that the body was subsequently found, and reburied.

Some elements in the Toldoth narrative that seem utterly foreign to the conventional view of Jesus' life are actually supported by a few tantalizingly brief and seemingly insignificant passages in the canonical New Testament. The detailed account in the Toldoth of Jesus' first arrest, and subsequent escape, seems at first to be a strange embellishment. Yet on closer examination, this incident appears to be confirmed by John 10:39, which says much the same thing, although with extreme brevity: "Therefore they sought again to take him, but he escaped out of their hand." John's observation that the Jews were picking up stones to throw at Jesus suggests that the situation may well have been one of immediate peril, as it is in the Toldoth; yet this incident is not mentioned at all in the Synoptic Gospels. The Toldoth has the followers of Jesus picking up stones at this point, both accounts illustrating how extremely serious had become Jesus' challenge to what the Jews perceived as the rule of law.

JESUS' PURPORTED MIRACLES: MAGIC TRICKS?

The fable in the Toldoth of how Jesus supposedly performed miracles because he alone knew the "Ineffable Name" is hinted at by various passages of the New Testament. In Matthew 13:35, Jesus says, "I will utter things which have been kept secret from the foundation of the world." In Matthew 8:16 Jesus "cast out the spirits with his word." Revelations 19:11-16 clearly suggests Jesus' use of the "Ineffable Name": "and he had a name written, that no man knew, but he himself." And "he hath on his vesture and on his thigh a name written, KING OF KINGS AND LORD OF LORDS"; we recall that in the Toldoth Jesus secretes the "Ineffable Name" in the flesh of his thigh. In Greek legend Zeus cut into his thigh in exactly the same manner to hide away and nurture his unborn son Dionysus when the child's mortal mother was consumed by fire.

The story in the Toldoth of Jesus' animation of the clay birds, which seems at first to be yet another fanciful invention, is in fact an event which, while escaping mention in the canonical Gospels, is confirmed by other ancient texts. In fact, this event is mentioned twice in the Koran, the Islamic holy text written in the seventh century. Jesus is recognized as a prophet by the religion of Islam; hence we find accounts of him in their text. In Surah 3:49 of the Koran, Jesus says, "Lo! I fashion for you out of clay the likeness of a bird, and I breathe into it and it is a bird, by Allah's leave." The miracle is mentioned again in Surah 5:110. This story also appears in the "apocryphal" Christian Gospel of Thomas. Schonfield suggests that Matthew 10:29-31 may be a remnant of this story, where Jesus says, "Are not two sparrows sold for a farthing? and one of them may not fall on the ground without your father"; in the Toldoth, the animated birds soon fall back to earth. But this seems unlikely, since Jesus' parable of the birds turns out to be a restatement of an older saying in the rabbinical literature.[13] If we recall that the art of magical illusions traces back to Egypt, long before the time of Jesus, and that magicians then, as now, performed tricks with concealed doves, we can envision how an illusion might be performed to make clay birds to seem to come to life.

The account of the life of Jesus in the Toldoth is not, of course, without serious problems. There was no "Queen Helene" of Judea at the time of Jesus, or at any other time. Schonfield suggests that what now reads "Queen Helene" was in the original manuscript "Herod the Tetrarch," which would indeed be correct, although the foundation for that supposition is unclear.

Schonfield does not tell us where this "Queen Helene" might be found, but a queen of that name is well known in Jewish history. The *Jewish Encyclopedia* describes "Queen Helena of Adiabene, the illustrious and munificent proselyte to Judaism." Queen Helena's best-known contribution to Jewish life seems to have been to attempt to reinstate "the ordeal" for adultery (see Numbers 5:12–31) at a time when creeping Greco-Roman licentiousness had made adultery and fornication so common that they scarcely seemed worth making a fuss about. Queen Helena presented to the Temple, as a subtle reminder, a golden tablet inscribed with the appropriate chapter of "the Law," to be used for the rite of this ordeal.[14] If at the time the Toldoth was written the name "Queen Helena" had become synonymous with "getting tough on adulteresses," the use of her name in the Toldoth may have been intended as a wry comment on the conduct of Jesus' mother. It is also possible that there is no real significance to the name: the author of the Toldoth may have simply been in error, confusing one well-known Jewish monarch with another. Such confusions are not unknown in the rabbinic literature.

Another matter we cannot possibly take seriously is the account of the theft of the "Ineffable Name," nor what Jesus is alleged to have been able to do with it. We likewise cannot take seriously the account of the world's first human aerial combat, between Jesus and Judas Iscariot. Schonfield notes the parallels between this account and the legendary aerial confrontation between St. Peter, founder of the orthodox church, and Simon Magus, reputed founder of Gnosticism. Magus was said to have demonstrated his devilish powers by flying into the air, but the apostles Peter and Paul are said to have sent him crashing to the ground by their prayers.[15] Why a variant of this story should have apparently found its way into the Toldoth is problematical.

The many reputed faith healings and even resurrections also cannot, of course, be explained logically *if* we accept the accounts at face value. It should suffice to note, however, that even in our own time, when information travels much faster and farther than it did twenty centuries ago, the very same claims are being widely made by Christian evangelists, and are widely believed by their flock. But whenever the matter has been rigorously investigated, the claim has invariably turned out to be unsubstantiated.[16] Hence, it is not necessary to possess the "Ineffable Name" or any *genuine* healing powers whatsoever to get a substantial following as a faith healer, even today. The author of the Toldoth, as a God-fearing rabbi, no doubt must have concluded that since so many people claimed these remarkable things to have actually occurred, the only way they possibly could have occurred was by the misuse of the "Ineffable Name." We can observe the process of rationalization at work in the Toldoth, as in so many other religious texts. If Jesus worked miracles, he must have stolen his powers from the Jews. If Paul led the Christian sect to break completely with Judaism, the Jews must have arranged this themselves to be rid of them. And so on.

We must keep in mind the circumstances in which the Toldoth was composed. It reflects the orthodox Jewish viewpoint, and was written by a rabbi. Schonfield places its origin in the rabbinical school in Tiberias, located on the Sea of Galilee, sometime during the fourth century A.D. It was written from an orthodox viewpoint: not only was Jesus a heretic and a fomenter of rebellions, but an ill-behaved and disrespectful illegitimate child; whatever powers he may have possessed must have been stolen from the Temple. Of course, from our twentieth-century perspective we understand how easily crowds can be impressed by the appearance of "miracles," since "faith healers" and magical entertainers perform similar feats every day. Hence we need not resort to imaginings about the "Ineffable Name" to explain *reports* of miracles. For upon close examination, such reports invariably turn out to be grossly inaccurate, or to have omitted significant information that would allow one to explain away the "miracle."

What the Toldoth undoubtedly represents is an attempt by Jews to tell *their side* of the story of Jesus. At the time it was set down in its present form, Christianity was emerging triumphant, having become the official religion of the Roman Empire. The Toldoth represents the attempt by Jewish religious authorities to preserve the story of Jesus as *they* understood it. "You Christians are preaching your Gospels throughout the world: but we say it happened this way." It is the attempt of an embattled people to preserve what *they* believed to be the facts behind a highly significant and controversial story in which they play a major role. The Toldoth is the only surviving book from antiquity to tell the anti-Christian side of that momentous, world-historical controversy in the first century of our era. The following chapters demonstate how the perspective of the Toldoth illuminates the process by which Christianity, a religion having its origin among those resentful of the rule of Jewish law, shaped itself into the preferred expression of proletarian resentment in the ancient world, a tool custom-crafted for ending the rule of Rome.

NOTES

1. Epistle of Athanasius: see *The New Columbia Encyclopedia* (1975 ed.), s.v. "New Testament." Athanasius and the Gnostics: see Elaine Pagels, *The Gnostic Gospels* (New York: Vintage Books, 1981), chapter 6.

2. Hugh J. Schonfield, *According to the Hebrews* (London: Duckworth, 1937), p. 207; R. Joseph Hoffmann, *Jesus Outside the Gospels* (Buffalo, N.Y.: Prometheus Books, 1984), p. 50.

3. Voltaire, *Dictionnaire philosophique* (1764), s.v. "Messie" (Messiah) and "Christianisme."

4. Origen, *Contra Celsum* 2:27. Origen's self-mutilation is related by Eusebius in his *Ecclesiastical History* 6:8. Of Origen, Eusebius writes, "The saying 'there are eunuchs who made themselves eunuchs for the kingdom of heaven's sake' [Matthew 19:12] he took in an absurdly literal sense."

5. Nietzsche, *Der Antichrist* (1888), 45.

6. Schonfield, *According to the Hebrews*, p. 74.

7. Ibid., p. 72.

8. Ibid., p. 24.

9. Ibid., pp. 106–13.

10. Talmud, Yeb. iv, 13: quoted by Schonfield, *According to the Hebrews*, p. 139; Jesus as "that man": *The Jewish Encyclopedia* (ca. 1905), s.v. "Jesus."

11. Talmud: tractate Sanhedrin 43a: quoted by Schonfield, *According to the Hebrews*, p. 157; Acts of John: Schonfield, *According to the Hebrews*, p. 171.

12. "The earliest and best manuscripts [of Mark] lack the last twelve verses printed in the King James version and conclude the Gospel with the words, 'for they were afraid' (xvi:8)." Bruce Manning Metzger, in the article "Gospels," *Collier's Encyclopedia* (1978 ed.)

13. Schonfield, *According to the Hebrews*, pp. 90–92, 169–70. Bultmann has demonstrated the non-originality of Matthew 10:29, as well as many other "sayings" attributed to Jesus: see William Barclay, *Introduction to the First Three Gospels* (Philadelphia: The Westminster Press, 1975), p. 54.

14. *The Jewish Encyclopedia*, s.v. "Adultery."

15. See E. Cobham Brewer, A *Dictionary of Miracles* (Philadelphia: J. B. Lippincott Company, 1884), p. 218.

16. For an in-depth investigation, and ultimately definitive refutation, of the claims made about virtually every major contemporary faith healer, see William Nolen, *Healing: A Doctor in Search of a Miracle* (New York: Random House, 1974): James Randi, *The Faith Healers* (Buffalo, N.Y.: Prometheus Books, 1988).

2

The Birth of Christianity
from the Spirit of Resentment

> ". . . I will destroy the wisdom of the wise,
> and will bring to nothing the understanding
> of the prudent. . . . God hath chosen the
> foolish things of the world to confound the
> wise; and God hath chosen the weak things
> of the world to confound the things which
> are mighty. . . ."
>
> 1 Corinthians 1:19,27

Envy and resentment are terribly corrosive passions. To suffer at the sight or even the thought of others' enjoyment of life makes one a committed enemy of human happiness. Such people end up being practically a curse upon the human race. They vandalize life, exerting themselves not in the pursuit of gain or pleasure, but to hinder others' enjoyment. (The worldview of the resentful is the subject of my previous book, *Resentment Against Achievement* [1988].)

Religion exists as a powerful force in most contemporary human societies because it fulfills a very fundamental need: the need for hierarchy inversion. The lives of many of those at the bottom of every society are tormented by a burning envy and hatred of those above them, whose all-too-visible success so obviously contrasts with the squalor that fills their own lives. This generates a seething resentment which any generosity on the part of the affluent serves merely to inflame, a sense of brooding malice that renders many of the poor too angry to act in their own economic self-interest. It does not matter whether these people are at the bottom because of prejudice and tradition, or because of their own lack of productivity, discipline, and self-control. Whatever the reason, they will carry around a powerful grudge against those whose lives are joyous. Those for whom life has been befouled by the consequences of their own envy, nurture a sullen and spiteful maliciousness against those who enjoy comfort, fulfillment, and sexual satisfaction. They become the implacable enemies of anything that is well-constituted.

Today most people do not even know what "envy" means, because we no longer have a word to express this concept. If we think of "envy" at all, we conceive of it as something trifling and inconsequential. We say "I envy you," as if "envy" were a synonym for "admiration." But before the time of the French Revolution, "envy" was understood as something far more malicious. The word derives from the Latin *invidere*, signifying the "harmful stare" of the envious as they contemplate with envenomed eyes the success of others more disciplined than themselves.[1] In virtually every society, the "evil eye" so feared by the superstitious is popularly associated with envy; those who envy us stare with so much malice that it seems to some that their very gaze possesses the magical power to inflict harm. To envy means not merely to covet others' possessions, but includes the desire to harm them out of spite; the envious derive pleasure from denigrating the successful or vandalizing their possessions. Ovid and Shakespeare knew envy to signify not "admiration," but an emotion that renders one sick, green, and repulsive. Ovid's personification of Envy, in his *Metamorphoses*, has been called "the most repulsive figure of Greco-Latin mythology," and his verses on it "the most damning poetic sentence on any passion."[2] Steeped in putrefaction, Ovid's Envy is more repulsive than even the Gorgon. Showing a similarly keen insight, Shakespeare's Romeo bids Juliet,

> Arise, fair sun, and kill the envious moon,
> who is already sick and pale with grief,
> that thou her maid art far more fair than she:
> Be not her maid, since she is envious;
> Her vestal livery is but sick and green
> And none but fools do wear it; cast it off . . .
>
> (*Romeo and Juliet*, II.2)

When the revengeful instincts of the proletariat are ineffectively restrained, it results in great physical carnage at the hands of a Robespierre, or Stalin, or Hitler, or Pol Pot. But because society's laws usually hold such murderous anger firmly in check, proletarian vengefulness is ineffectual until it eventually becomes creative enough to move into the spiritual realm. The result of this is a Tertullian, or Savanarola, or Calvin, or Khomeini, or Jim Jones. When too weak to inflict physical vengeance on those whose pleasures cause them to suffer the pains of acute envy, the resentful revel in the destructiveness of an angry God powerful enough to cause the destruction that they themselves cannot, and experience great vicarious glee imagining the suffering awaiting those who now are happy. When such religious fanatics are able to seize and hold power, they are too impatient to postpone until the afterlife the torments that infidels are supposed to suffer, and begin inflicting torments while the latter are still on earth. This clearly demonstrates that it is not piety or beneficence, but the desire to inflict punishment, that propels the fanatics of such movements.

TERTULLIAN AND CHRISTIAN VENGEFULNESS

Perhaps the clearest example of the delight in revenge of the Christian worldview is seen in this passage of Tertullian (ca. 160–225 A.D.), one of the most influential and revered Fathers of the Christian Church. In his work *de Spectaculis* (*On Spectacles*), Tertullian comments wryly on the Roman public's passion for grand spectacles:

> You are fond of spectacles—expect the greatest of all spectacles, the last and eternal judgment of the universe. How shall I admire, how laugh, how rejoice, how exult, when I behold so many proud monarchs, and fancied gods, groaning in the lowest abyss of darkness; so many magistrates, who persecuted the name of the Lord, liquefying in fiercer fires than they ever kindled against Christians; so many sage philosophers blushing in red-hot flames with their deluded scholars; so many celebrated poets trembling before the tribunal, not of Minos, but of Christ; so many tragedians, more tuneful in the expressions of their own sufferings; so many dancers. . . .[3]

Here we see, in undiluted form, the potent spirit of vengefulness that gave birth to the Christian church. Centuries of rising secularism have, of course, diluted and weakened this venom, allowing more positive elements to work their way to the front, but the religion still carries around the remnant of this destructive anger. It lies frozen in its sacred texts like an insect trapped in amber. In the above passage, Tertullian expresses his fervent desire to humiliate and torture the most celebrated achievers of his day: philosophers and poets, scholars and dancers, whose anticipated destruction he celebrates. Not merely the accomplished will be destroyed, but the powerful as well: monarchs along with their magistrates, and even the dead and deified emperors, would be tormented unceasingly.

In this metaphysically complete hierarchy inversion, the mighty will be brought low and punished for having once been high, while the once lowly will be exalted, their triumph made a thousand times sweeter by the delight of watching those they once envied writhing below them in eternal suffering. In fact, St. Thomas Aquinas explicitly states, "In order that the bliss of the saints may be more delightful for them and that they may render more copious thanks to God for it, it is given to them to see perfectly the punishment of the damned."[4] In this resentment-based system of morality, anything that is well-constituted or successful is deserving of destruction, precisely *because* it is successful, while true holiness dwells solely in things that wallow in sickness, venom, impotence, or filth. Thus Aquinas teaches that the shameful emotion the Germans call *schadenfreude*[5]—literally, "shadow joy," a secret delight in seeing the misery of others—is actually a virtue under Christian morality.

One might point out in Tertullian's defense that many Christians were being tormented and killed in the Romans' infamous public "spectacles," martyrs to their faith (although Gibbon persuasively notes that the number of those persecuted is not nearly as large as the church has led us to believe). Thus some might say that Tertullian's desire for revenge was "justified." But consider what a wide swath Tertullian's anger sought to cut! All revenge is, strictly speaking, pointless brutality, except perhaps when intended as a deterrent to future offenders; once a violent act is committed, it can never be undone, no matter how severe the retribution against the offender. Setting this objection aside, one could scarcely blame Tertullian if he had sought vengeance against the magistrate who had ordered some particularly hideous persecution, or against the executioner who carried it out. One could even argue that Tertullian might have been justified in trying to assassinate the cruel Roman emperor who had ordered this savage persecution of Christians. But see how *wide* is the scope of his vengeance! Tertullian sought revenge not merely against certain parties guilty of cruel acts, but against *anyone* and *anything* that was respected. The very concept of respectability and success was being attacked. We find this same urge for destructiveness in the underclass today, in their delight in vandalizing persons and property, and their perverse refusal to subordinate themselves to perform productive work. Expressing the resentment inherent in the proletarian's ethics, Tertullian sought to spoil *the very enjoyment of life itself*, pouring out venom and guilt upon all earthly pleasure, no matter how innocent.

ST. AUGUSTINE

In a similar vein, St. Augustine laments being distracted in his de-votions by watching a lizard catching flies. One might think that there is nothing inherently sinful about watching lizards out of the corner of one's eye. However, Augustine correctly notes that his interest in such things is a snare of the world, diverting his attention from Things Beyond. Augustine is even bothered by the necessity of eating, seeing food as a seduction to pleasure, and he ardently wishes that there could be some method of begetting children without succumb-ing to "lust."[6] Thus to the early Christians all "things of the world" were depicted as horrid instead of pleasant, and life itself degraded from an exuberant pursuit to a dreary, perilous preparation for a promised better life to come.

Christianity's opposition to the fulfillment of life was well known to the *philosophes*, those philosophers of the Age of Reason. They criticized Christianity not merely because they believed its doctrines to be contrary to reason, but because of its fanatical intolerance and its spirit of hostility toward intellectual inquiry. Voltaire wrote that "every sensible man, every honorable man, must hold the Christian sect in horror."[7] His friend and colleague Denis Diderot wrote a parable about a man who was so embittered by life that he retired to a cave to ponder how he might inflict the greatest possible degree of misery and vengeance upon those around him. He later emerged from the cave shouting "God! God!"[8]

FRIEDRICH NIETZSCHE ON CHRISTIAN RESENTMENT

However, the link between Christianity and resentment was not made explicit until 1886, when Nietzsche wrote *The Genealogy of Morals*.

In it Nietzsche first uses the term *ressentiment*—a French word essentially identical in meaning to the English "resentment"—to designate a state of outrage resulting from the perception of another's position of superiority relative to oneself. This superiority may be manifested in any attribute that is valued in life—money, status, power, or sexual attractiveness—and those who are angered by their relative lack of these things secretly become the implacable enemy of those whose lives are richer than theirs. Nietzsche characterizes those given over to *ressentiment* as "physiological distortions and worm-riddled objects, a whole quivering kingdom of burrowing revenge, indefatigable and insatiable in its outbursts against the happy, and equally so in disguises for revenge, in pretexts for revenge."[9] He explicitly identifies Christian morality as a manifestation of *ressentiment*. Nietzsche had a great deal to say about *ressentiment* in all his subsequent works; he obviously considered it to be among his most important ideas.

The thrust of *The Genealogy of Morals* is precisely what the name implies: it is an attempt to trace the origins of the systems of morality that have prevailed at various places and times. This is the first book that dared to ask the question, *What is the value of values?* In other words, what is the benefit or harm to an individual or a group from holding a particular moral code? Some moralists believe moral values to have been handed down from "on high" by supernatural beings. Others view them as arbitrary human inventions, with no reason to prefer one over any other. But Nietzsche viewed moral codes as presupposing aims and intentions, and suggested that we not only can— but *must*—compare the relative worth of moral codes by examining the intention behind each, and the likely result. Moral codes can be evaluated by examining the consequences of that code to those who hold it. Nietzsche sought to determine what traits were common to those moral codes that allowed one to survive and prosper, and what traits in a code of values caused it to imperil one's survival. He determined that Christianity clearly fell into the latter category, as did socialism. He urged upon scholars the urgent task of "the determination of the *order of rank among values*."[10] Just at a time when many moralists were beginning a gradual slide into a relativism or even nihilism concerning moral values, Nietzsche acknowledged the moral vacuum, then joyously set out finding ways to fill it.

The Genealogy of Morals consists of three essays. In the first essay Nietzsche contrasts the concepts of "good and evil" with "good and bad." He had dealt with this subject to some extent the previous year, in his famous *Beyond Good and Evil*. However, Nietzsche soon realized that the first work had fallen far short of clearly explaining his ideas, and started working on *The Genealogy of Morals*, covering the same ground, but with more directness.

The code of morality of a healthy, vibrant society, Nietzsche states, derives primarily from the successful experiences of its leaders. They typically pretend that their own moral code was handed down by some deity in order to give it greater authority. But this phase of a civilization does not last forever. Sooner or later those who cannot assert their "will to power" via meaningful actions attempt to do so by creating a set of values that is wantonly destructive. "The slave revolt in morality begins when *ressentiment* itself becomes creative and gives birth to values: the *ressentiment* of natures that are denied the true reaction, that of deeds, and compensate themselves with an imaginary revenge." Nietzsche notes that "these weak people—some day or other *they* too intend to be the strong . . . to experience that one needs to live a long time, beyond death." [11]

In the second essay of the same volume, Nietzsche observes that "all instincts that do not discharge themselves outwardly *turn inward*— this is what I call the *internalization* of man." [12] This passage profoundly influenced Sigmund Freud, who expanded it into the extremely influential notion of the "repression" of human instincts. (No matter what problems exist in other areas of Freud's theories, it is clear that he— and Nietzsche—were quite correct in this matter.) Nietzsche held that those who are troubled by "guilt" and "bad conscience," whose origins he saw in the recognition of one's indebtedness to others, eventually come to interpret their "animal instincts as a form of guilt before God." Nietzsche views the attempt to repress or deny one's instincts as "sickness, beyond any doubt, the most terrible sickness that has ever raged in man." [13]

The third and final essay of *The Genealogy of Morals* deals with "The Meaning of Ascetic Ideals." Continuing his earlier theme, Nietzsche observes that "the sick represent the greatest danger for the healthy; it is not the strongest but the weakest who spell disaster for the strong." He views "the most malicious of all conspiracies" as being that of "the suffering against the well-constituted and victorious." In his view, Christianity was part of this conspiracy. Much duplicity is employed, warns Nietzsche, in attempting to disguise the nature of that hatred by "the mendacious failures whose aim is to appear as 'beautiful souls.' " Their ultimate hope, he asserts, is in "poisoning the consciences of the fortunate with their own misery." Nietzsche urges the healthy to remain at as great a distance as possible, both physically and psychologically, from these suffering as-cetics.[14]

Because the psychologically healthy cannot nurse these sick ones back to health—that would only result in the contagion of suffering—there arises "the necessity of doctors and nurses *who are themselves sick*; and now we understand the meaning of the ascetic priest." Thus the ascetic priest is the natural shepherd and advocate of "the sick herd"; were it otherwise, the two could not understand each other. The priest defends his "sick herd" against its own malice, disintegration, and anarchy, keeping it from destroying itself. However, as he does this, "the most dangerous of all explosives, *ressentiment*, is constantly accumulating." The priest must therefore find a safety valve for this anger, to keep it from exploding. Nietzsche expresses the priest's solution most succinctly: "the priest *alters the direction of ressentiment.*"[15] This powerful negative energy may be directed, in whole or in part, at some outsider whom it is convenient to despise, or back at the sufferer himself, in the form of guilt. In other words, Nietzsche discerned that the role of the ascetic priest is to tell his suffering flock *whom to hate* and whom to blame for the misery of their lives.

Seldom has an idea so startling and significant been so directly stated. When a group of unhappy people is burning with *ressentiment* at the sight of others' success, the job of the priest is to direct that venom outward, to prevent the self-destruction of his group. Thus Tertullian urged Christians to despise "the worldly"; Hitler told un-happy Germans that Jews were to blame; Lenin and Stalin told im-poverished peasants to blame greedy capitalists for their privation, while the Ayatollah Khomeini and Saddam Hussein urged impov-erished religious fanatics angered by modernity to hate that "Great Satan," America. Today racist "skinheads" tell poor white people to blame all their problems on blacks, while Black Muslims urge unhappy blacks to blame white people, especially Jews.

In each instance, the principle is the same: a leader—Nietzsche's "ascetic priest"—unites and motivates a group of suffering people by directing its *ressentiment* outward at some convenient target, thereby diverting a venomous anger that otherwise might well be directed at the priest's own position in the hierarchy. Unfortunately, as the priest fans the flames of *ressentiment*—or, in Nietzsche's phrase, "infects the wound"—he is adding fuel to the very fire that must go out before the groups' problem can be solved. The priest, by inculcating and incubating the resentments of his flock, perpetuates the very problem that caused their suffering in the first place.

THE RELIGIOUS CHANNELING OF RESENTMENT

Thus we see how religion and superstition *do* fill a need for many people, although it is an ultimately destructive one. The various priests, rabble-rousers, and witch-doctors direct deep-seated resentments into socially approved channels. This prevents the envy and resentment of the miserable from being directed against the priest who does the channeling, and perhaps absolving kings or commissars in the process. This can be invaluable in situations where *overcoming* such resentments is not even remotely possible; it is, however, an emergency pressure-release, and only worsens the problem in the long term. Thus, the typical Moslem religious fanatic is a seething mass of violent resentments, ready to strike out and kill Americans, blasphemers, and any other designated instruments of Satan. If some well-to-do foreigner were to suggest to him, however timidly, that he consider doing something that doesn't strike his fancy, he would immediately rise up in heated defiance, and the foreigner would be lucky to escape with his skin. Yet this same surly, noncompliant ruffian is routinely manipulated by his own religious hierarchy like a marionette on strings. They tell him what to say, what to do, and what to think; *yet he harbors not the slightest hint of resentment against their total dominance over his life.* How is this possible? Nietzsche would say that the Mullahs have done their job well, deflecting the fanatic's rabid *ressentiment* from themselves to outsiders.

The same is true to a lesser degree of Christian fundamentalists. The hardscrabble poor farmer of the rural South, bursting with populist resentment against "big banks," "big business," and "egghead intellectuals," expresses not the slightest degree of envy of the wealth of successful members of his own church, and shows no evident resentment of the tremendous degree of control the clergy exercises over his life. This channeling of the sufferer's resentments quite effectively vaccinates the fundamentalist against infection by socialist or feminist resentments, both of which are highly poisonous to any society they infect. Indeed, the absence of feminist *ressentiment* allows the birthrate in religious societies to remain well above the zero-growth level, in an era when reproduction in most groups in virtually all industrialized countries has resulted in negative growth. While this may not seem immediately significant, should the trend continue for a century or two, these fundamentalist groups will be populous and thriving, while the urban-feminist liberals will have gone the way of the Shakers. It is not yet generally recognized that feminism, like socialism, is a self-limiting form of *ressentiment*, one leading slowly but inevitably to the dominance via Darwinian selection of some other form of social organization that is more fit to perpetuate itself over long periods of time.

But the religious fanatic purchases these advantages at a terrible cost. Such xenophobia against "the Infidel" makes it impossible for one to function effectively in a large, diverse marketplace, one in which people of many creeds and nations participate freely. Given current trends in global economic development, any nation or group whose xenophobia limits its participation in worldwide technology, education, and trade will remain at a great disadvantage compared to those whose cosmopolitanism does not. A far better solution than allowing powerful resentments to develop, and channeling them, is for a society to rise as far as is possible above every form of resentment and envy. This requires that people learn to recognize manifestations of these destructive passions, and that when encountered they must be soundly and universally denounced. Educated people have already learned to reject immediately and decisively all manifestations of racism and religious bigotry. We must reach the point where displays of envy and of resentment against achievement elicit the same response.

NIETZSCHE'S *ANTICHRIST* AND THE NEGATION OF THE WILL TO LIVE

Two years after completing *The Genealogy of Morals*, Nietzsche penned the most devastating and complete philosophical attack on Christian psychology, Christian beliefs, and Christian values ever written: *Der Antichrist*.[16] It was one of the last things he ever wrote. Unlike the confusing allegories and symbolism of Nietzsche's *Zarathustra*, there can be no mistaking the language or the intention of *Der Antichrist*, a work of exceedingly clear prose and seldom equaled polemics. Even today, the depth of Nietzsche's contempt for everything Christianity represents will surprise and shock many people, and not only devout Christians.

Nietzsche begins *Der Antichrist* by sketching the idea of declining versus ascending life and culture. An animal, a species, or an individual is "depraved" or "decadent" when it loses its instincts for that which sustains its life, and "*prefers* what is harmful to it." Life itself presupposes an instinct for growth, for sustenance, for "the will to power," the striving for some degree of control and mastery of one's surroundings. Christianity sets itself up in opposition to those instincts, and hence Christianity is an expression of decadence, a negation of the will to life.[17]

Nietzsche explains that the pessimistic philosophy of Arthur Schopenhauer is, like Christianity, decadent. Schopenhauer taught that since it is impossible to satisfy the desires of the will, one must ceaselessly renounce striving for what one wants, and become resigned to unhappiness. In the late nineteenth century Schopenhauer's doctrines were extremely popular, especially among the Wagnerians. Richard Wagner's monumental *Tristan und Isolde* is a powerful expression of Schopenhauerian pessimism as the lovers sing of the impossibility of earthly happiness, and of their anticipated mystical union in the realm of "night" after their death. The opera closes with Isolde's famous *liebestod*, or "love-death." She sings of a vision of her dead lover gloriously and mystically transfigured up there in the heavenly regions, then she ecstatically dies to join him.

Nietzsche charges that Christianity denigrates the world around us as mere "appearance," a position grounded in the philosophy of Plato and Kant, and hence invents a "completely fabricated" world of pure spirit. However, "pure spirit is pure lie," and thus the theologian requires one to see the world falsely in order to remain a member in good standing in the religion. The Christian outlook was, Nietzsche says, immensely bolstered against the attacks of the Enlightenment by Immanuel Kant, whose philosophy renders reality unknowable. (For Kant a virtue is something *harmful* to one's life, a view Nietzsche could never accept. If we *want* to do something, Kant would say our action cannot possibly be virtuous; any action that contains an element of self-interest is by Kant's definition not virtuous.) Nietzsche summarizes the Kantian morality: "*anti-nature* as instinct, German decadence as philosophy—that is Kant."[18]

Returning to the theme of Christian doctrine as misrepresentation, Nietzsche charges that "in Christianity neither morality nor religion come into contact with reality at any point." The religion deals with imaginary causes (such as God, soul, spirit), imaginary effects (sin and grace), and the relationships between imaginary beings (God, souls, and angels). It also has its own imaginary natural science (wholly anthropomorphic and non-naturalistic), an imaginary human psychology (based on temptation and repentance), as well as an imaginary teleology (apocalypse, the Last Judgment, the kingdom of God). Nietzsche concludes that this "entire fictional world has its roots in the hatred of the natural" world, a hatred which reveals its origin.

For "who alone has reason to *lie himself out* of actuality? He who *suffers* from it."[19] Here is the proof that convinced Nietzsche that Christianity is not only decadent in its origins, but rotten to its very core: no one reasonably satisfied with his own mind and abilities would wish to see the real world replaced with a lie.

Comparing religions, Nietzsche came to the conclusion that a healthy society's gods represent the highest ideals, aspirations, and sense of competence of that people. For example, Zeus and Apollo were obviously powerful ideals for Greek society, an image of the mightiest mortals projected into the heavens. Such gods are fully human, and display human strengths and weaknesses alike. The Christian God, however, shows none of the normal human attributes and appetites. It is unthinkable for this God to desire sex, food, or even openly display petty vengefulness (as did the Greek gods). Such a God is clearly emaciated, sick, castrated, a reflection of the people who invented him. If a god symbolizes a people's perceived sense of impotence, he will degenerate into being merely "good" (an idealized image of the kind master, as desired by all slaves), void of all genuinely human attributes. The Christian God represents the "divinity of decadence," the reduction of the divine into a God who is the contradiction of life. Those impotent people who created such a God in their own image do not wish to call themselves "the weak," so they call themselves "the good."[20]

Nietzsche compares Christianity to Buddhism. Both, he says, are religions of decadence, but Buddhism is a hundred times wiser and more realistic. Buddha does not demand prayer or asceticism, demanding instead ideas that produce repose or cheerfulness. Buddhism, he says, is most at home among the higher and learned classes, while Christianity represents the vengeful instincts of the subjugated and the oppressed. Buddhism promotes hygiene, while Christianity repudiates hygiene as sensuality. Buddhism is a religion for mature, older cultures, for persons grown kindly and gentle—Europe is not nearly ripe for Buddhism. Christianity, however, tamed uncivilized barbarians, subjugating wild "*beasts of prey*," who cannot control their own "will to power." The way Christianity did this was to make its adherents sick, making them thereby too weak to follow their destructive instincts. Thus Buddhism is a religion suited to the decadence and fatigue of an ancient civilization, while Christianity was useful in taming barbarians, where no civilization had existed at all.[21]

Nietzsche places special emphasis on Christianity's origin in Judaism, and its continuity with Jewish theology. He was fond of pointing out the essential Jewishness of Christianity as a foil to the anti-Semites he so despised, effectively taunting those who hate the Jews: Why did you adopt their religion? It was the Jews, he asserts, who first falsified the inner and outer world with a metaphysically complete anti-world, one in which natural causality plays no role. (One might of course object that such a concept considerably predates Old Testament times.)

The Jews did this, however, not out of hatred or decadence, but to survive. The Jews' will for survival is, Nietzsche asserts, the most powerful "vital energy" in history; he admired those who struggle mightily to survive and prevail. As captives and slaves of more powerful civilizations—the Egyptians and the Babylonians—the Jews shrewdly allied themselves with every "decadence" movement, with everything that weakens a society, not because they were decadent themselves, but in order to weaken their oppressors. Thus, Nietzsche views the Jews as shrewdly inculcating guilt, resentment, and other values hostile to life among their oppressors as a form of ideological germ warfare, taking care not to become fully infected themselves. This technique was ultimately successful in defeating mighty empires—Babylonians, Egyptians, and Romans—by in essence making them "sick," and hence less powerful. (The Romans, of course, succumbed to the *Christian* form of Judaism, in this view.) This parallels St. Augustine, quoting Seneca, who says that the Jews "have imposed their customs on their conquerors."[22]

"On a soil *falsified* in this way, where all nature, all natural value, all *reality* had the profoundest instincts of the ruling class against it, there arose Christianity, a form of mortal hostility to reality as yet unsurpassed." The revolt led by Jesus was not primarily religious, says Nietzsche, but was instead a secular revolt against the power of the Jewish religious authorities. The very dregs of Jewish society rose up in "revolt against 'the good and the just,' against 'the saints of Israel.' " This was the political crime of Jesus, a crime of which he was surely guilty, and for which he was executed. Nietzsche examines the psychology of Jesus, as much as is possible from the biblical accounts, and detects a profound sense of withdrawal: "Resist not evil, the kingdom of God is within you." He sees parallels between the psychology of Christ and Dostoevsky's *The Idiot*. (Dostoevsky is not mentioned here by name, but Walter Kaufmann writes, "It seems plain that Nietzsche conceived of Jesus in the image of Dostoevsky's *Idiot*.")[23]

Nietzsche deduces that the earliest Christians sought to retreat into a state of extreme withdrawal from "the world," undisturbed by reality of any kind. They rejected all strong feelings, favorable or otherwise. Their fear of pain, even in infinitely small amounts, "cannot end otherwise than in a religion of love." Thus Nietzsche sees early Christianity as promoting an extremely dysfunctional state resembling autism, a defense mechanism for those who cannot deal with reality. Noting Christianity's claims to "deny the world," and its stand in opposition to every active virtue, Nietzsche asks how any person of dignity and accomplishment cannot feel *ashamed* to be called a Christian?[24]

Surprisingly, Nietzsche expresses some degree of admiration for the character of Jesus, at least the manner in which he faced his death. Jesus expressed no bitterness or hostility toward those who arrested and tormented him, and did not seek to have his followers avenge his death. He was *above* every such form of vindictiveness, and died graciously in order to convince others of the correctness of his manner of living.[25] Certainly Roman Stoic philosophers would have had to admire Jesus' courage in facing death, assuming that the gospel account represents real historical fact.

Christ's disciples, however, were not as willing to forgive. In Nietzsche's view, the very worst of them was Paul, the actual founder of much Christian doctrine. Nietzsche was convinced that Paul was not sincere in his beliefs, that "*his* requirement was *power.*" Nietzsche cannot bring himself to believe that Paul, "whose home was the principal center of Stoic enlightenment," is sincere when he offers up a hallucination as proof that the Redeemer still lives. Paul invented the doctrines of "eternal life" and "the Judgment" as a means to his ends. In *Die Morgenrote*, or *Daybreak*, Nietzsche had earlier discussed Paul's frustrations at being unable to master, and to comply with, Jewish law, and hence Paul "sought about for a means of destroying" that law. Christianity offered Paul just the weapon he had been seeking.[26]

By placing the center of life outside of life, in "the beyond," Nietzsche says Christianity deprives life of any focus or center whatsoever. The invention of "the immortal soul" automatically levels all rank in society: " 'Immortality' conceded to every Peter and Paul has so far been the greatest, the most malignant attempt to assassinate *noble* humanity." Thus "little prigs and three-quarter madmen may have the conceit that the laws of nature are constantly broken for their sakes," thereby obliterating all distinctions grounded in merit, knowledge, or accomplishment. Christianity owes its success to this flattering of the vanity of "all the failures, all the rebellious-minded, all the less favored, the whole scum and refuse of humanity who were thus won over to it." For Christianity is "a revolt of everything that crawls upon the ground directed against that which is elevated: the gospel of the 'lowly' *makes* low."

Here we clearly see Nietzsche's repudiation of Christianity's attitudes as well as its theology: as he pointedly noted in *Ecce Homo*, "no one hitherto has felt Christian morality beneath him." All others saw it as an unattainable ideal.[27] Pre-Christian thinkers did not, of course, see poverty as suggestive of virtue, but rather of its absence. One point Nietzsche was unable either to forgive or forget was that the enemies of the early Christians were "the intelligent ones," persons far more civilized, erudite, and accomplished than themselves, people whom Nietzsche believed far more fit to rule than were Christians.

Nietzsche views the gospels as proof that corruption of Christ's ideals had already occurred in those early Christian communities. They say "Judge Not!" then send to Hell anyone who stands in their way. Arrogance poses as modesty. He explains how the New Testament typifies the morality of *ressentiment:* "Paul was the greatest of all apostles of revenge."[28] (This was written before the time of Hitler, Lenin, Stalin, and Pol Pot. Today, the awarding of that title might not be so automatic.)

At this point, Nietzsche advises the reader to "put on gloves" when reading the New Testament, because one is in proximity to "so much uncleanliness." It is impossible, he says, to read the New Testament without feeling a partiality for everything it attacks. The Scribes and the Pharisees must have had great merit, to have been attacked by the rabble in such a manner. Everything the first Christians hate has value, for theirs is the unthinking hatred of the rabble for everyone who is not a wretched failure like themselves. Nietzsche sees Christianity's origins in what Marxists would call "class warfare," and sides with those possessing learning and self-discipline against those having neither.[29]

THE WAR BETWEEN SCIENCE AND RELIGION

Nietzsche next turns to a point essential for the understanding of his thought: the inevitability of a "warfare" between Christianity and science. Because Christianity is a religion that has no contact with reality at any point, it "must naturally be a mortal enemy of 'the wisdom of the world,' that is to say, of *science.*" Here "science" is not to be understood as merely the physical sciences, but as any rigorous and disciplined field of human knowledge, which is a potential threat to any rigid dogma. Hence Christianity must calumniate the "disciplining of the intellect" and intellectual freedom, bringing all organized secular knowledge into disrepute. For "Paul *understood* the need for the lie, for 'faith.'" Nietzsche refers to the Genesis fable of Eve's temptation, asking whether its significance has really been understood: "God's mortal terror of science?" The priest perceives only *one* great danger: the human intellect unfettered. Continuing the metaphor of science as eating from "the tree of knowledge": "Science makes godlike—it is all over with priests and gods when man becomes scientific. Moral: science is the forbidden as such—it alone is forbidden. Science is the *first* sin, the *original* sin. *This alone is morality*: 'Thou shalt not know'—the rest follows." The priest invents and encourages every kind of suffering and distress so that man may not have the opportunity to become scientific, which requires a considerable degree of free time, health, and an outlook of confident positivism. Thus, the religious authorities work hard to make and keep people feeling sinful, unworthy, and unhappy.[30]

Christianity, says Nietzsche, needs sickness as much as Hellenism needed health. (To understand this point, compare a Greek statue of a tall, handsome, naked god with a Christian religious image of an unhygienic, slovenly figure suffering greatly.) One does not "convert" to Christianity, but rather one must be made "sick enough" for it. The Christian movement was, from its beginning, "a collective movement of outcast and refuse elements of every kind," seeking to come to power through it. "In hoc signo *decadence* conquered." Christianity also stands in opposition to intellectual, as well as physical, health. To doubt becomes sin. "'Faith' means not *wanting* to know what is true,"[31] a description that strikes me as stunning, and quite exact.

Nietzsche now turns to consider *why* the lie is told. Once again, Christian teachings are compared to those of another religion, the Indian book of Manu, "an incomparably spiritual and superior work." Unlike the Bible, the *Law Book of Manu* is a means for the "noble orders" to keep the mob under control. Here, human love, sensuality, and procreation are treated not with revulsion, but with reverence and respect. After a people acquires a certain experience and success in life, its most "enlightened," most "reflective, and far-sighted class" sets down a law summarizing its formula for success in life, which is represented as a revelation from a deity, for it to be accepted un-questioningly. Such a set of rules is a formula for obtaining "hap-piness, beauty, benevolence on earth." This aristocratic group considers "the hard task a privilege . . . life becomes harder and harder as it approaches the heights—the coldness increases, the responsibility in-creases." All ugly manners and pessimism are below such leaders: "indignation is the privilege of the Chandala" (Indian untouchable). What is bad? "Everything that proceeds from weakness, from revengefulness."[32]

Thus Nietzsche holds that the *purpose* for the lie of "faith" makes a great difference in the effect it will have on society. Do the priests lie in order to preserve (as in the book of Manu, and presumably Greek myth), or to destroy (as in Christianity)? Thus the early Christians and socialist anarchists are identical in their instincts: both seek solely to destroy. The Roman civilization was a magnificent edifice for the prosperity and advancement of life, "the most magnificent form of organization under difficult circumstances which has yet been achieved," which Christianity sought to destroy *because* life prospered within it. These "holy anarchists" made it a religious duty to destroy "the world," which actually meant, "destroy the Roman Empire." They weakened the Empire to such an extent that even "Teutons and other louts" could conquer it. Christianity was the "vampire" of the Roman Empire. These "stealthy vermin," shrouded in night and fog, crept up and "sucked out" from everyone "the seriousness for true things and any instinct for reality."[33] Christianity moved truth into "the beyond," and with the beyond one negates life.

Before charging Nietzsche with possibly irresponsible invective, compare the above with Gibbon's summary of the role of Christianity in *The Decline and Fall of the Roman Empire*:

> The clergy successfully preached the doctrines of patience and pusil-lanimity; the active virtues of society were discouraged; and the last remains of a military spirit were buried in the cloister: a large portion of public and private wealth was consecrated to the specious demands of charity and devotion; and the soldiers' pay was lavished on the useless multitudes of both sexes who could only plead the merits of abstinence and chastity.[34]

On the positive side, Gibbon notes that even though Christianity clearly hastened the demise of Rome, it "mollified the ferocious temper of the conquerors." But overall, Gibbon seems to parallel Nietzsche's view that Christianity seeks to control the uncivilized not by teaching them the self-discipline needed to control their own impulses, but by making them too "sick" to do a great deal of harm.[35]

"The whole labor of the ancient world in vain": thus does Nietzsche overstate the magnitude of the calamity. (Our civilization's heritage from classical antiquity is obviously far from nothing!) Nonetheless, no one who prefers civilization to barbarism can be indifferent to the point here raised. Nietzsche emphasizes that the foundations for a scholarly culture, for science, medicine, philosophy, and art, had all been magnificently laid in antiquity, only to be destroyed. Today, he says, we have certainly made great progress, but each of us still retains decadent habits and instincts which we must work hard to overcome. Two thousand years ago, we had acquired that clear eye for reality, patience, attention to detail, seriousness in even small matters—and it was not obtained by "drill" or from habit, but flowed naturally from a civilized instinct. All this was lost! And it was not lost to some natural disaster or destroyed by "Teutons and other buffaloes" (Nietzsche's contempt for German nationalism and militarism knew no bounds!), but it was "ruined by cunning, stealthy, invisible, anemic vampires. Not vanquished—merely drained. Hidden vengefulness, petty envy become master." Everything that was miserable and filled with bad feelings about itself came to the top at once.[36]

The meaning and significance of the Renaissance is considered in the next-to-last section of Der Antichrist. "The Germans have cheated Europe out of the last great cultural harvest which Europe could still have brought home—that of the Renaissance." Nietzsche views the Renaissance as "the reevaluation of Christian values," i.e., the repudiation of life-denying Christian values and their replacement with secular values emphasizing art, culture, and learning. With the Renaissance in Italy, Christianity was being repudiated at its very seat. "Christianity no longer sat on the papal throne! Life sat there instead!" Nietzsche envisions the immortal roar of laughter that would have risen up from the gods on Mount Olympus had Cesare Borgia actually succeeded in his ruthless quest to become pope. (The notorious murderer and poisoner Borgia, the son of Pope Alexander VI, spread his power ruthlessly across Italy. Father and son appointed or poisoned cardinals as required to engineer the son's election to the papacy. However, the plan went awry when they accidentally tasted some wine that had been "prepared" to rid themselves of a wealthy cardinal! The father died, and the son became gravely ill, and was hence in no position to coerce the selection of his father's successor.)[37]

Nietzsche laments that this great world-historical event—*life* returning to Western culture—was ultimately undone by the work of "a German monk," Martin Luther, who harbored the vengeful instincts of "a failed priest." Through Luther's Reformation, and Catholicism's answer to it, the Counter-Reformation, Christianity was restored.[38] One might be tempted to dismiss Nietzsche's dramatic interpretation of the Renaissance, xcept that his view matches that of Jacob Burckhardt, the single most influential historian of Renaissance civilization who ever lived. Burckhardt's monumental work, *The Civilization of the Renaissance in Italy* (1860), has influenced the study of that period as much as Gibbon's *Decline and Fall* did that of ancient Rome.

Nietzsche and Burckhardt were colleagues at the University of Basle, and friends as well. In the first section of his *Civilization*, Burckhardt writes that the greatest danger ever faced by the papacy was its secularization during the Renaissance. "The danger that came from within, from the popes themselves and their *nipoti* (relatives; compare our word "nepotism"), was set aside for centuries by the German reformation. . . . The moral salvation of the papacy was due to its mortal enemies. . . . Without the reformation—if indeed it is possible to think it away—the whole ecclesiastical state would have passed into secular hands long ago." Pope Julius II, powerfully anti-Borgia, was "the savior of the papacy," who put an end to the practice of the buying and selling of Church positions. However, the Counter-Reformation "annihilated the higher spiritual life of the people," according to Burckhardt. Nietzsche would have said this was because they had become *Christian* once again.

CONCLUSION

Thus we now understand the function played by a religion of resentment, and why its tenacity is so great—far greater than that of any older polytheistic religion. It provides a formula by which life's losers can proclaim to the happy, "you *have not* won!" It asserts the metaphysically certain victory of pain, of guilt and other bad feelings, over all worldly joy, self-reliance, all exuberance and success. All those who are pained by life exult in such a religion of *ressentiment*, while those who enjoy life must suffer it as a burden. It hands the resentful a cosmic monkeywrench to toss in the plans of achievers. Clearly, Islam plays a similar role in delaying the modernization of Middle Eastern cultures. All achievement-oriented persons are denounced as "worldly," and are accused of being in league with Satan. Thus Islam today, like the Christianity of centuries gone by, allows the rage and envy of those whom life is passing by to impede directly and effectively the progress of those whose innovations and energy drive civilization forward.

Because *ressentiment* seems to be an ineradicable vice of the human race, like violent aggression, lying, and theft, it makes no sense to hope for a "final victory" over all such religions. For resentment will always be with us. But if we learn to recognize such metaphysical vandalisms for what they are, the slander of life by those pained by it, they will cease to work such an effect.

In the chapters that follow, we will see why those at the bottom of society joined the new religion of Christianity, and why for centuries the religion remained almost entirely that. We will see what force seems to have impelled Jesus' rebellion against the religious hierarchy, and why so many others among the "downtrodden" were enthralled by his successes. Not until we understand the powerfully disapproving social forces bearing down upon one such as Jesus of Nazareth can we understand why he and his disciples acted as they did. It will then be clear why things had to turn out as they did: why the Roman world witnessed the Birth of Christianity from the Spirit of Resentment.

NOTES

1. See the *Oxford English Dictionary* (1933 ed.), s. v. "envy."

2. Ovid, *Metamorphoses*, Book II, The Tale of Mercury and Herse. "The most repulsive": de la Mora, *Egalitarian Envy* (New York: Paragon House, 1987), p. 16.

3. Tertullian, *De Spectaculis* 30, trans. Edward Gibbon, from chapter XV of *The Decline and Fall of the Roman Empire*.

4. Aquinas, *Summa Theologica*, III, *Supplementum*, Q. 94, Art. 1. See a discussion of this in Nietzsche, *Genealogy of Morals* I.15.

5. See Helmut Schoeck, *Envy* (New York: Harcourt, Brace, & World, 1970).

6. Augustine: the snare of the lizard, gossip, and "the lust of the eyes": *Confessions* 10.35; eating as a seduction to pleasure: *Confessions* 10.31; wishing that "the organs of parenthood, too, might function in obedience to the orders of will and not be excited by the ardors of lust": *City of God* 14:16.

7. Quoted by Peter Gay in *The Enlightenment: An Interpretation. The Rise of Modern Paganism* (New York: Alfred A. Knopf, 1966), chapter 7.

8. Diderot, *Philosophic Thoughts*, part 15.

9. Friedrich Nietzsche, *The Genealogy of Morals* III. 14. For an enlightening discussion of Nietzsche's concept of *ressentiment*, and its further development by Max Scheler, see Schoeck, *Envy*, chapter 11.

10. Nietzsche, *The Genealogy of Morals* I. 17.

11. Nietzsche, *Genealogy of Morals* I. 10, I. 15.

12. Nietzsche, *Genealogy of Morals* II. 16. For Nietzsche's influence on Freud, see Walter Kaufmann, *Nietzsche* (Princeton, N.J.: Princeton University Press, 1974), chapter 7.

13. Nietzsche, *Genealogy of Morals* II. 22.

14. Nietzsche, *Genealogy of Morals* III. 14.

15. Nietzsche, *Genealogy of Morals* III. 15.

16. There are two excellent English translations of *Der Antichrist* readily available, one by R. J. Hollingdale (Penguin Classics, 1968), the other by Walter Kaufmann (in Kaufmann's *The Portable Nietzsche* [Penguin Books, 1978]).

17. Nietzsche, *Der Antichrist* 6.

18. Nietzsche, *Der Antichrist* 8–11.

19. Nietzsche, *Der Antichrist* 15.

20. Nietzsche, *Der Antichrist* 16–19.

21. Nietzsche, *Der Antichrist* 20–22.

22. Nietzsche, *Der Antichrist* 23–26; Augustine, *City of God* VI. 11.

23. Kaufmann, *Nietzsche*, chapter 12.

24. Nietzsche, *Der Antichrist* 27–30, 38.

25. Nietzsche, *Der Antichrist* 31–40.

26. Nietzsche, *Der Antichrist* 40–42; *Morgenrote*, trans. R. J. Hollingdale (Cambridge University Press, 1982), 68.

27. Nietzsche, *Der Antichrist* 43; *Ecce Homo* 4 ("Why I Am a Fatality"), 8.

28. Nietzsche, *Der Antichrist* 44–45.

29. Nietzsche, *Der Antichrist* 46.

30. Nietzsche, *Der Antichrist* 47–49.

31. Nietzsche, *Der Antichrist* 51–52.

32. Nietzsche, *Der Antichrist* 57.

33. Nietzsche, *Der Antichrist* 58–59.

34. Gibbon, *Decline and Fall of the Roman Empire*, chapter XXXVIII.

35. Ibid.

36. Nietzsche, *Der Antichrist* 59.

37. This saga of the Borgias is in Part One of Jacob Burckhardt, *The Civilization of the Renaissance in Italy* (New York: Mentor, 1960), pp. 112–13.

38. Nietzsche, *Der Antichrist* 60.

3

The Making of the Messiah, Part One: The Cruci-fiction

> ". . . For Christ sent me not to baptize, but
> to preach the gospel: not with wisdom of
> words, lest the cross of Christ be made of
> none effect. . . ."
>
> 1 Corinthians 1:17

The New Testament is a book which is best understood when not read in the usual order, from start to finish. That was a sequence chosen by the proponents of the religion, one that places their story in its best light. When read in that sequence, it is almost impossible to see how the New Testament *evolved*. Like a living organism, the teachings and doctrines of Christianity underwent evolution by Darwinian pressures, resulting in the survival of those stories that were the most fit to attract and hold crowds, and to meet objections. The books are understood most clearly when read chronologically, from the oldest epistle to the latest gospel, from the simplest to the most sophisticated, from straightforward simplicity to sophisticated duplicity. To gain the clearest insight into the origin and psychology of Christianity, I would suggest starting one's investigation with the Toldoth, which we have already examined, in which some details of Jesus' life have been "frozen," without benefit of later Christian emendation. I would next read the genuine Pauline and other early epistles, then the Acts of the Apostles, and then the Gospels: first Mark, then Matthew, then Luke, and finally John. Next, Revelations, and finally those pseudo-Pauline and other late epistles that are a product of a relatively mature theology: 1 and 2 Timothy, Titus, 2 Thessalonians, Ephesians, and Hebrews, and all remaining books.

The reason for this somewhat strange-sounding suggestion is to highlight one's awareness that the non-gospels are *very* different kinds of works from the gospels themselves. They are obviously far more primitive, especially the early epistles, and far less specific than the gospels. In those New Testament books outside the gospels, we learn absolutely nothing about the earthly origins of Jesus. The apostles seem to know nothing on this subject themselves; they strangely fail to make any mention of any "virgin birth" in their Acts, Revelations, and various epistles. Only in the final two of the three Synoptic Gospels is this proclaimed, after its fortunate "discovery" by the influential Bishop of Antioch late in the first century.

Except in the first chapter of Acts, in verses that are probably at least as late as the Gospels of Luke and John, Jesus' mother, Mary, is never mentioned. The non-gospels contain practically nothing in the way of details of the events of Jesus' life; Peter, Paul, James, Jude, and John do not seem to know a great deal about what Jesus said or did. They do not discuss his sermons or his teachings in any detail. There is no notion of the Trinity, of Original Sin, the Virgin Birth, or any other late enhancement to the religion. There is much vague talk about "grace" and "righteousness" and "repentance," but next to nothing is said about the specific actions and events so artfully described in the gospels. Why Paul did not mention the details of some of these remarkable things in his letters to his churches is puzzling. The epistles speak in general terms about Jesus being "raised up" from the dead—Paul always uses the passive voice—yet the authors seem to know nothing whatsoever about the events that are claimed to have followed the Resurrection: the meetings between the risen Christ and his apostles, Jesus convincing doubting Thomas, eating a fish, and rising up to Heaven after forty days on earth.

The authors of some of the earliest books scarcely even seem to know that Jesus is supposed to have been crucified, and they certainly do not seem to know any of the events that putatively occurred at the crucifixion. The early books are almost as likely to say that Jesus was "slain and hanged on a tree" as that he was crucified. It strikes me as extraordinarily odd that Paul, who for years supposedly had Luke at his side when writing letters to his various far-flung churches, evinces practically no knowledge of the supposed "facts" that later went into a gospel said to have been written by Luke. Likewise Peter, who says he witnessed the sufferings of Christ, says Jesus was hung on a tree.

Citing this same paucity of detail in the earliest books of the New Testament, G. A. Wells deduces from them that Jesus never existed, but was instead a legendary being about whom stories grew over time.[1] Wells is indeed correct to deduce the growth of fictitious elements from this strange paucity of early details. I would suggest, however, a less extreme explanation for the early books being so vague on the details of Jesus' life: many of those details are embellishments invented to meet later objections raised against the church's teaching, and had *not yet been made up* at the time that some of Acts, and many epistles, were written. I personally do not doubt that one "Jesus of Nazareth" was a real first-century figure. So many nearly contemporary writings mention him, some quite flatteringly, while others are exceedingly hostile. Imaginary figures do not engender such divisiveness. No ancient Jewish text expresses the slightest doubt as to Jesus' real existence. Jesus seems to have had real flesh-and-blood relatives; there is little reason to doubt that James, known as "The Just," was actually Jesus' brother, although probably a half-brother. In the earliest Christian communities, those who were relatives of Jesus were known as *desposyni*, giving them much prestige. The grandsons of Jude, Jesus' other brother, were personally interrogated, then released, by the emperor Domitian around the year 90.[2] Ironically, the most persuasive proof of Jesus' historicity may be the strident tone of hostility in the rabbinical writings any time Jesus' name is mentioned, or even alluded to. This "Jesus of Nazareth" *must* have been a real person to have left the rabbinical establishment in such a stew. Whatever it was he did, he drove them into a state of near-apoplexy. No merely mythological being is ever surrounded by such spirited partisans, both pro and con.

THE FORMATION OF THE CANONICAL NEW TESTAMENT

We recall that the Roman philosopher Celsus, writing around the year 170, charged that by the time he was writing, the Christians had already "corrupted the Gospel from its original integrity, to a threefold, and fourfold, and manifold degree, and have remodeled it, so that they might be able to answer objections." It is the aim of the next three chapters to show exactly how that corruption and remodeling has taken place.

Among the liturgical books that have been used in Christian worship, even in Roman churches, are many that were removed from the Canon when the New Testament was standardized by St. Athanasius in 367. (This is the same Bishop Athanasius who firmly established the Christian doctrine of the Trinity; were it not for his tireless efforts and lobbying, the Godhead might today consist of two Divine Persons, or a single Divine Person, or perhaps even four!)[3] These discarded books are today known as the "apocrypha" of the New Testament. Most of them, however, were never "lost" in any real sense, although many were not generally available until the twentieth century. These books were not necessarily dropped from the Canon because they were felt to be "wrong," or not inspired by God, but rather that they were inappropriate for worship, or unnecessary. Several epistles among the "apocrypha" are of undoubted authenticity and of great historical value, making them documents of incomparably greater merit than certain pious pseudonymous fabrications retained in the canonical New Testament. Several of the "apocryphal" books seem to have been dropped primarily because they require too much energy to be expended in their defense. For example, two Gospels of the Infancy of Jesus were deleted, in spite of attesting to many fine miracles, probably because in them Jesus is depicted as spiteful and destructive. When a boy runs into him in the street, Jesus strikes him dead. The dead boy's family comes to Jesus' house to complain, and Jesus strikes them blind. Joseph soon comments to Mary, "Henceforth we will not allow him to go out of the house; for everyone who displeases him is killed."[4] It is easy to see why the Infancy Gospels were dropped from the Canon; such petulance makes Jesus look as vengeful as Zeus or Apollo. We will later see why other once holy books became inconvenient, and were subsequently removed to the Church's attic.

The three Synoptic Gospels—Matthew, Mark, and Luke—are not only similar in content, but in many places contain nearly identical text. John, quite different in content and approach, derives from an independent tradition and source. With the exception of fundamentalists, who believe that the Bible was inerrantly dictated by God exactly as it now stands, and was probably proofread by Him as well, scholars are generally agreed that Mark is the oldest of the three

Synoptic Gospels. That conclusion seems inescapable, as Mark is indeed the shortest, and the simplest, of the three. It also contains the greatest number of theological problems that are missing from the other two. The language in Mark, while coherent, is simple and unpolished, and tends toward unnecessary repetition. That of Matthew is improved over Mark, while the language of Luke is elegant, gracious, and poetic, the highly polished work of an erudite and literate Greek.

The writing of the Gospel of Mark occurred only about forty years after Jesus' death, and it appears to have been written by someone who heard these events described by an eyewitness, perhaps even by a witness who played a role in the drama. The later Synoptics are more distant from the events they depict, both in years, and in the number of persons who must have participated in the chain of transmission. For that reason alone their accuracy is more suspect. Matthew and Luke are believed by most scholars to have been derived by combining the material in Mark with some otherwise unknown source of information about Jesus, designated as Q. Some scholars think there may be one or more other ancient sources, especially in Luke, and have termed this L. These sources are said by some to be oral traditions of the sayings and events of Jesus' life, and some such compilation of Jesus' sayings may well have existed.

The two late Synoptics add, of course, far more to Mark than just "the sayings of Jesus," and the doubter may rightfully demand to know from whence this information came, and what assurance we may have that it is credible. The cynic justifiably harbors suspicions that Q and L consist primarily of "fancy" and "invention," respectively, being whatever material was needed to meet the objections being raised against Mark. Indeed, the noted biblical scholar James M. Robinson writes that when the demythologizing efforts of David Strauss and other nineteenth-century scholars had seemingly undermined the historical credibility of both the Synoptic and Johannine Gospels, "the new answer to the question of the sources was the so-called Two-Document Hypothesis, to the effect that the traditions shared by Matthew and Luke were derived from two relatively old and reliable sources they both used: the Gospel of Mark and a collection of sayings today called Q. This theory was generally regarded as a liberation from Strauss."[5] In other words, the Two-Document Hypothesis was invented as a defense against the findings of critical analysis by those who wanted to take the Synoptics literally, attempting to make the later-produced Synoptic material seem credible. (If any Catholics are reading this, they must be warned that they do so at the peril of their immortal souls, for the Papal Biblical Commission ruled in 1912 that Catholics may not freely defend the two-source hypothesis of the gospels.[6] It is recommended that Catholics read these next three chapters with their eyes closed.)

Thus the major additions, and minor revisions, to the gospels were not made to incorporate new material as it became available. Rather, we must reemphasize that they were made to *be better able to respond to objections* raised against Christian teachings by pagans and Jews. The Synoptic Gospels reached their current state by this process of sequential "improvement," or, to use terms more appropriate to biblical scholarship, "higher forgery." By inventing new material specifically designed to meet the principal objections being raised against the gospel bearing the name of Mark, they could then "discover" a new gospel, and attribute it to Matthew. After all, you cannot take a gospel which is in widespread use in the liturgy and make wholesale revisions to it, without explanation. Such a move would appear far too crude; we must remember that as the Christian faith became more widespread, even though it was primarily embraced by the rude, the ignorant, and the credulous, there were at least some converts among educated and sophisticated persons, who would notice—and object to—such open chicanery.

But we *can* fortuitously "discover" a new gospel, saying much the same thing as the current one does, but which explicitly addresses those problems that are currently the most troublesome. We can then let the old gospel fall into disuse, which in a time when books are rare will cause it to fade from the memories of the faithful. This latter scenario is precisely what happened to Mark. "The Greek text of Mark has not been greatly altered in transmission. Though it was popular for a generation and then fell into considerable neglect (until rescued by the Four-Gospel Canon in the middle of the second century), its very neglect saved it," as B. H. Streeter pointed out.[7]

Thus, Matthew was written not to *add* to the account in Mark, but to *replace* it. Later still, by making more changes to Matthew, a third gospel can be "discovered," and attributed to Luke, fixing those problems still remaining, and polishing up the story stylistically to make it more appealing to an upscale audience. The author of Luke likewise may have hoped that his gospel would replace the earlier two: he begins it: "Forasmuch as many have taken in hand to set forth in order a declaration of those things which are most surely believed among us . . . it seemed good to me also, having had perfect understanding of all things from the very first, to write unto thee in order, most excellent Theophilius. . . ." The author of Luke seems to be saying, "Pay no attention to what Mark and Matthew have written—I alone know the *real* story of Jesus!"

After at least a half-century had passed, later churchmen, perhaps themselves not knowing the real reason that Mark had been shelved, and now knowing of the existence of the Gospel of John, decided on a Four-Gospel Canon. (There is no evidence that the authors of the Synoptics knew of the Gospel of John. There appears to be some evidence for the converse, although the dependency of John upon the Synoptics cannot be very great.) The author of each of the Synoptics expected that only one gospel would be used in the churches, the one he was writing. It was probably when the Gospel of John turned up in widespread use in churches in the Eastern Mediterranean that the effort to shape and control public knowledge of the life of Jesus solely via the evolution of the Synoptic Gospels was abandoned.

A careful examination of the sequence of "improvements" to Christian texts, especially the Synoptic Gospels, reveals the kinds of problems the Evangelists faced in attempting to preach the Gospel of Christ to a critical audience. Their phenomenal success is as great a tribute to their dedication and ingenuity as it is an indictment of their lack of scruples. The level of moral turpitude characteristic of television evangelists today probably accurately conveys the dismally low ethical standards prevailing among their evangelical counterparts nineteen centuries earlier.

THE FIRST MAJOR FABRICATION: THE "CRUCI-FICTION"

Early Canonical Accounts

The first significant change in the story of Jesus involved altering the circumstances of his death. Instead of teaching that Jesus had been slain and hanged on a tree, which was apparently the earliest story and is what probably happened, the Evangelists changed the story to say that he was nailed to a cross. We recall from the last chapter that there are several New Testament passages outside the gospels that quite literally tell us that Jesus was slain and hanged on a tree:

Acts 5:30:   "Jesus, whom ye slew and hanged on a tree"

Acts 10:39:   "whom they slew and hanged on a tree"

Acts 13:29:   "they took him down from the tree"

1 Peter 2:24:   "who his own self bare our sins in his own body
                   on the tree"

Galatians 3:13:   "Christ . . . being made a curse for us . . .
                   Cursed is every one that hangeth on a tree"

Each of these passages employs the same Greek word *xulon*, literally "wood." In the New Testament and other early Christian writings, this word is frequently used to suggest the living wood of a tree. This same word is used to represent "the tree of life" (Revelations 22:2), and the "green tree" in Luke 23:31, which is contrasted in that passage with "dry" wood (*xeron*). So, clearly, to the Greek-speaking early Christians, *xulon* would be understood to mean the wood of a living tree. Its etymology suggests the branching arms of a tree. Another peculiar word describing Christ's punishment is used in Acts 2:23 (from a speech by Peter), as is the "tree" of Acts 5:30; while translated as "crucified," it literally means "fastened" (*prospēgnumi*), which is more suggestive of hanging than crucifixion.

Gospel references to Jesus' "cross" or "crucifixion" in the original Greek imply that he had been "impaled" on an upright stake (*stauros* > the verb *stauroō*). Frank Zimmerman writes, "It is extraordinary that *xulon* goes flatly against the tradition of the Four Gospels which use *stauros* and *stauroō*, 'cross' and 'crucify,' over fifty times and do not once mention hanging on a tree."[8]

All the Jewish accounts—various Talmudic passages as well as the Toldoth—are absolutely consistent in having Jesus "slain and hanged in a tree." The Koran, while accepting Jesus as a prophet of Allah, likewise denies that Jesus was crucified, although it does not say whether he was hanged. Unfortunately, we do not seem to know precisely what the prophet Muhammad maintained did happen to Jesus, nor do we know for sure what sources he may have used for this information. (His information *may* have come directly from Allah; then again, it may not.) The Koran is somewhat ambiguous on the subject of Jesus' death. Surah 4:156–57 has the Jews saying, "We slew the Messiah Jesus, son of Mary, Allah's messenger—They slew him not nor crucified, but it appeared so unto them . . . they slew him not for certain, but Allah took him up unto Himself."

The *Shorter Encyclopaedia of Islam* states, "it is certain that Muhammad rejected the crucifixion and accepted the ascension."[9]

Christian apologists claim, of course, that the references to "the tree" are supposed to be a favorite "metaphor" of the cross used by the early evangelists. That explanation might convince us if we did not know that to be "slain and hanged in a tree" was decreed by Jewish law as the punishment for religious offenders.

Nowhere in any of the gospels does it say that Jesus was "hanged," or was ever on a "tree"; New Testament writers must have abruptly lost their fondness for this "metaphor" ere Mark set reed to papyrus. Some scholars date the Acts of the Apostles as not much later than the year 60. "There is no sign in the Acts of any later sources [than 61], or any reference to later events or conditions. . . . The evangelization of Syria . . . in the form in which it appears in Acts, ends with the Jerusalem Council in 49."[10]

Assuming this to be correct, and assuming that the "hanged in a tree" passages are from the older parts of Acts, then all references to Jesus "hanging in a tree" are older than the first gospel.[11] This suggests that the "party line" on this matter changed sometime after Paul started writing, but before Mark did. Thus the cruci-fiction story is older than the oldest gospel, but not as old as the oldest New Testament passages: it must have been invented somewhere between about 50 and 70.

I realize that this significant revision of Christian history and dogma will seem to many extreme, perhaps even absurd. But given the tantalizing hints we see of this in Acts and the earliest epistles; given the explicit account in Jewish writings; and given the other, more unmistakable, changes in Christian "history" that have been made by the early evangelists, it seems extremely probable, even if it cannot be proved as a certainty, that Jesus was not crucified, but was literally "slain and hanged on a tree."

Capital Punishment under Rabbinic Law

The Jews executed transgressors either by stoning, burning, beheading, or strangulation, depending on the offense; burning was very rare. We find a reference to an adulteress about to be stoned in John 8:3–11. While New Testament scholars recognize that this passage was grafted onto John at a later date,[12] adultery was indeed sometimes punished by stoning. There are numerous references to stoning offenders in the Old Testament; the King James Concordance lists twenty-nine references in the Old Testament to offenders being "stoned," or to the verb "to stone." As for hanging the body of the offender on a tree afterward, this is approved in Deuteronomy 21:22–23, provided that the body is taken down by nightfall. It was a long-standing practice in Jewish law that no punishment could be inflicted unless it was sanctioned in the Scriptures,[13] and there is ample scriptural precedent for offenders being "slain and hanged in a tree." Joshua hanged the king of Ai on a tree, taking the body down by nightfall (Joshua 8:29). In Esther 2:23, two men who have plotted against the king are likewise hanged in a tree. Others in the Old Testament are also hanged, although not necessarily in trees. The victim, already dead, is not hanged by the neck; instead he is suspended by his hands which are tied together above his head. If the Jews executed Jesus by crucifying him, they would have repudiated their laws by doing so!

It is often said that the Jews arrested Jesus, then turned him over to the Romans for execution. But in 1 Thessalonians 2:14–15— an undoubtedly genuine letter of Paul, and probably the oldest book in the entire New Testament—it very plainly states that Jesus was killed by the Jews. "For ye also have suffered things of your own countrymen, even as they have of the Jews: who both killed the Lord Jesus, and their own prophets, and have persecuted us."[14] Assuming this to be correct, Jesus could not possibly have been crucified. The Jewish council of law, the Sanhedrin, was composed of grave and godly men who had sworn solemn oaths to follow strictly the dictates of Scripture, and of rabbinic law, which prescribed the interpretation of scriptural commands. There is absolutely nothing in Jewish law or custom to suggest that it is possible to arrest a prisoner, convict him, then turn him over to some other group for execution. Hiam Cohn, a noted Israeli jurist, writes: "It is inconceivable that a Jew would be delivered by a Jewish court to the Roman enemy for execution, whatever his crime; the Sanhedrin would rather have abstained from passing capital sentences than having them carried out by a hateful adversary in a manner incompatible with Jewish law and repellent to Jewish sentiment."[15] Whims and caprice played no role in Jewish judicial proceedings: if a course of action had no scriptural sanction, it was not to be performed. It is significant that Peter's accusation, "Jesus, whom ye slew and hanged on a tree" (Acts 5:30), is hurled at the Sanhedrin, the very group that *would* have hanged Jesus on a tree, if such were done.

According to *The Jewish Encyclopedia*, the death penalty was eliminated entirely in the year 40, when Jewish courts were stripped by the Romans of their authority to inflict capital punishment.[16] (It might appear that the Romans, as in Gilbert and Sullivan's *Mikado*, were unhappy at not seeing as many executions performed as they might like to preserve order, and decided to take the matter into their own hands.) Thus the Jews still retained this authority at the time Jesus was executed, approximately 29–33, although not for very many years afterward. In John 18:31, Pilate tells the Jews to deal with Jesus according to their own law, but they reply to him, "It is not lawful for us to put any man to death." This would explain why Jesus had to be executed in the Roman, not the Jewish, manner, even though it was the Jews, not the Romans, who clamored for his death. However, if *The Jewish Encyclopedia* is accurate, the Jewish court still could order executions in the year 30, and if it could not, Pilate should certainly have known that. Hiam Cohn states that at the time of Jesus' death, and even beyond, "the Sanhedrin did carry out capital sentences itself."[17]

The historian Josephus chronicles an incident occurring about 48 B.C. in which Herod, while he was governor of Galilee, created an uproar by executing some bandits without first giving them a fair trial before the Sanhedrin. It was universally objected by the Jews that under "our law" it is "forbidden to slay any man, even though he were a wicked man, unless he had been first condemend to suffer death by the Sanhedrin, yet hath [Herod] been so insolent as to do this."[18] A defiant Herod was himself called before the Sanhedrin to stand trial for murder. "But when Hyrcanus [the king] saw that the members of the Sanhedrin were ready to pronounce the sentence of death upon Herod, he put off the trial to another day, and sent privately to Herod, and advised him to flee out of the city."[19] This incident was, of course, some three generations before the execution of Jesus. Yet it shows how Jewish law jealously guarded its right to control the infliction of capital punishment, even under Roman rule.

In cases of idolatry or blasphemy, after the victim was dead, the body was hung on a gallows or in a tree (unless a woman), to serve as a warning to others. However, it had to be taken down by nightfall. Thus, from the sentence that was carried out against Jesus, we can infer that he must have been convicted by the Sanhedrin of idolatry or blasphemy. To be exact, he seems to have been accused as an "instigator to communal apostasy" (*maddiah*), a charge related to idolatry and carrying the same punishment.[20] The speed with which the execution of Jesus' sentence of death was carried out is likewise characteristic of Jewish, not Roman, law. Out of consideration for the victim, in order not to prolong his mental anguish, Jewish law required that the execution be carried out the same day the sentence was pronounced; to defer the execution was forbidden.[21] The Romans, by contrast, had no such requirement. Condemned persons often languished in dungeons for considerable periods of time, to be executed whenever a public spectacle was wanted. The fact that Jesus was taken out for immediate execution after the sentence was pronounced tells us that Jewish, not Roman, law was being followed.

The Talmudic Accounts

Several passages in the Talmud tell us quite plainly that Jesus was stoned to death. One would expect that Jewish writers would be only too happy to let the hated Romans take the blame for what later turned out to have been an extremely unpopular move, but such was not the case: all ancient Jewish accounts are consistent in having Jesus condemned by the Sanhedrin, slain, and hanged on a tree. Celsus likewise "seems to accept the familiar Talmudic tradition that Jesus was stoned, then hung up for display, on the eve of Passover."[22]

The Talmudic *Book of Sanhedrin*, in describing the type of evidence required to convict blasphemers "who are worthy of death according to the Torah," adds "and thus they did to Yeshu ben Stada in Lud; two disciples of the wise were chosen for him, and they brought him to the Beth Din [House of Judgment] and stoned him." Another Talmudic passage says, "the witnesses who hear from the outside bring him to the Beth Din and stone him. And thus they did to Yeshu ben Stada in Lud, and they hung him on the eve of Passover." Yet another passage says, "According to tradition, they hung Yeshu the Nazarene on the Eve of Passover." R. Joseph Hoffmann explains why Jesus is sometimes referred to as "ben Stada" in Jewish writings: "Stada" is actually "S'tath da," "she who went astray." Thus "ben Stada" is not, strictly speaking, a name, but an insult; Jesus is called "the son of the woman who went astray" in order to insult both him and his mother, who is consistently depicted in ancient Jewish texts as either a harlot or an adulteress. These rabbinical texts apply many interesting and unusual names to Jesus, all of them insulting. Now we understand why the Church forced the Jews to expurgate all passages dealing with Jesus or Mary. Sometimes Jesus is referred to as "Balaam," who in Numbers 24–25 seduced the Israelites into idolatry (and in Numbers 22 engaged in conversation with his ass).

Jesus is also sometimes called "Esau," who in Genesis 25:30–34 "despised his birthright." Sometimes Jesus' name is avoided altogether, and he is referred to obliquely as "that man," or "that anonymous one," or simply "bastard"; to pronounce a name was believed potentially to release great magic, and Jesus was widely regarded as a sorcerer.[23]

The Executions of Stephen and Matthew

The Acts of the Apostles gives us additional reason to doubt the Jews' impotence to carry out executions, the excuse offered in John for supposedly handing Jesus over to the Romans. Not long after Jesus' execution but before the conversion of Saul on the road to Damascus, a disciple of Jesus named Stephen is brought before the Sanhedrin, formally charged with blasphemy (Acts 6:11–12). He is tried in accordance with Jewish law. Witnesses are produced. The author says they are perjurers, but the important point is that a formal trial is occurring. Stephen gives a lengthy defense of his religious views, then at the end of chapter 7 he is taken out and stoned. The text implies, and many interpreters agree, that Stephen so angered the Sanhedrin that they simply halted the trial, dragged him outside and stoned him, without passing any formal sentence; indeed, if we are to maintain the cruci-fiction story, this is the only possible interpretation for the death of Stephen.[24]

But this is extremely implausible, as it implies that all these grave rabbis simultaneously decided to violate Jewish law, stop the trial, and lynch the accused! Because we first find Stephen being tried for a capital offense, and then find him suffering the penalty associated with that offense, the only reasonable conclusion is that he was found guilty of blasphemy by the Sanhedrin, with his execution taking place immediately after sentence was passed, exactly as prescribed by Jewish law. And if "it was not lawful" for the Sanhedrin "to put any man to death," why would they even try Stephen for blasphemy, for which the punishment *must* be death by stoning? We are not told whether Stephen's body was hanged in a tree until sundown, although according to law it should have been; we learn that "devout men carried Stephen to his burial" (Acts 8:2). Stephen thus became the first Christian martyr, his execution occurring after that of Jesus, but apparently before the year 40, when Jewish courts lost jurisdiction over capital punishment.

As if Stephen's execution did not cast enough doubt upon the cruci-fiction story, the Talmud tells us that Jesus' apostle Matthew likewise met his end by being condemned to death by the Sanhedrin![25]

The Execution of James

Hegesippus is one of the earliest non-canonical Christian writers from whom anything has been preserved. He wrote that "James the Just," the brother of Jesus, "suffered martyrdom like the Lord and for the same reason."[26] Since we know James to have been stoned to death for blasphemy, this passage implies that both brothers were tried for blasphemy by the Sanhedrin, found guilty, stoned to death, and hanged in a tree. A native of Palestine who wrote in the early second century, Hegesippus was one of Eusebius' main sources of information on the history of Jerusalem, and would have been in a good position to find out what really happened.

To the embarrassment of those who contend that only Roman courts in the first century held the authority for capital punishment, the historian Josephus records how James was brought before the Sanhedrin in what must have been 62, found guilty, and stoned. However, because this was a time of Jewish rebellion against Rome, the circumstances of this incident were not normal; Roman law had by this time overruled Jewish law on capital offenses, but Roman law was briefly usurped during the rebellion in 62. While in later centuries Christians freely altered and forged the works of Josephus, it is difficult to dispute the authenticity of this passage, since it was referred to by Origen, writing before the Christians came to power and were in a position to alter manuscripts. In the Nag Hammadi texts, lost until 1945, there is a remarkable account describing the stoning of James. This account of James' execution does indeed match the description in *The Jewish Encyclopedia* of how a stoning is supposed to be performed. (You do not simply pick up rocks and throw them!)[27]

COULD THE CRUCIFIXION HAVE HAPPENED?

Thus there are excellent reasons for doubting the story of Jesus' trial and crucifixion as related in the gospels. The gospel accounts of the trial, or trials, of Jesus, are not only mutually inconsistent, but appear to contain a great deal of fancy and invention. The *Encyclopaedia Judaica Jerusalem* says, "The Gospels in their present form contain descriptions of the so-called 'trial' of Jesus rewritten in a way making them improbable from the historical point of view."[28] R. Joseph Hoffmann writes that "the gospel story of the trial of Jesus is so filled with inaccuracies, however, that it cannot be held inherently more credible than the rabbinical accounts, which remember the trial of Jesus to have been a strictly *internal* affair, and his punishment for heresy stoning rather than crucifixion. . . . It should also be stressed that the Talmudic literature is absolutely silent concerning any Roman part in the trial and execution of ben Stada—a fact difficult to explain in view of the Christian willingness to (partially) exculpate the Jews. The consistency of the Talmud on this point should not be overlooked."[29] And the *Jerome Biblical Commentary*, which boasts a genuine *Ni il Obstat*, writes that the Marcan time framework of the cruci-fiction story has an "artificial" air about it (and we recall that it is from Mark's account that Matthew's and Luke's were drawn). "The impersonal tone of this section, the frequent use of the connective 'and,' the historical present in some verb forms, and the lack of any overly hortatory cast create the impression that the Evangelist writes not so much an eyewitness account as a compilation of details sifted from many stories about it in the early church."[30]

Many familiar Gospel details such as Jesus being led out slowly to the place of execution outside the city, being stripped of his clothes upon reaching the site, and being offered a soporific drink, are all part of the ritual associated with a victim being taken out for stoning.[31] Hiam Cohn, who explains in great detail why the Gospel accounts of Jesus' trial make absolutely no sense in either Jewish or Roman law, suggests that the Sanhedrin actually met "to prevent the crucifixion of a Jew by the Romans, and, more particularly, of a Jew who enjoyed the love and affection of the people."[32] Justice Cohn clearly was writing this with the laudable aim of improving relations between Christians and Jews, and his knowledge of law is truly encyclopedic. But I cannot accept his conclusion: the rabbinical accounts absolutely do not suggest that Jesus "enjoyed the love and affection of the people," that the rabbinical establishment would go out of its way to do Jesus a favor; nor do they suggest that the Romans played any role in the matter whatsoever. Regarding the jumbled and mutually contradictory sequence of events supposedly associated with the Roman trial and crucifixion of Jesus, one is left with the distinct impression that the confusion arises because these events never happened.

Where Is Calvary?

We face a marked problem in that the location of the supposed crucifixion—called "Golgotha" ("the Place of the Skull") or "Calvary"—
is unknown to geographers and historians. While the Church claims
to have discovered many relics associated with the Crucifixion, including the True Cross and the Holy Sepulcher, such discoveries are
only convincing when viewed with the Eye of Faith. The cross of
Jesus is said to have been located by a divine revelation, and authen-
ticated by its ability to animate a corpse.[33] Setting legend aside, there
is not now, and never has been, any such place as "Calvary." It is
indeed bizarre that the site of this historic event should be known
to the writers of gospels, but to absolutely nobody else. The Jerome
Biblical Commentary plaintively asks, in unfeigned astonishment, that
even after recognizing that Jerusalem was largely destroyed by the
Romans in the year 70, and again in 135, "is it likely that all memory of the area where this event took place would have disappeared
from the corporate consciousness of the early Christians?"[34] I would
agree that it is exceedingly unlikely that memory of the location of
such an event would have been lost—if the Crucifixion had been
a real event.

From a Jewish to a Roman Trial

In Mark, Jesus has two trials, a Jewish trial and a Roman one. Of
the two, the Jewish trial appears to be by far the more significant.
In fact, there seem to be two separate Jewish trials in Mark, a long
one following his arrest Thursday evening (Mark 14:53–64) and a
second one on Friday morning, recounted only very briefly (Mark
15:1). In Mark 14:63–64, the High Priest rends his garment as the
Talmudic interpretation of 2 Kings 18:37 requires him to do upon
hearing a blasphemy: "Ye have heard the blasphemy: what think ye?
And they all condemned him to be guilty of death." There is no
ambiguity whatsoever in what Jesus is charged with, or what his sentence should be. Discussing the verdict rendered in this passage, the
Jerome Biblical Commentary notes, "according to Leviticus 24 the penalty should have been stoning."[35] Furthermore, the sentence should
have been carried out immediately. It has been quite plausibly suggested that the reason a night and morning have been inserted in
the middle of the account of the Jewish proceedings (a night trial
is not supposed to occur) is to give Peter a chance to deny Jesus

three times before the cock crows. The Roman trial in Mark is exceedingly brief, just four short verses (Mark 15:2–5).

In Matthew 26:57–66, the Jewish trial of Thursday evening very much parallels that in Mark, although the significance of its result has been somewhat toned down. The high priest still rends his garment, and Jesus is pronounced to be "guilty" of blasphemy, but they stop short of actually condemning him. The Roman trial in Matthew 27:11–14 remains brief, and is nearly identical to that in Mark. However, by the time we get to loquacious Luke, the Thursday evening Jewish trial has almost disappeared completely. It now seems to be only a preliminary examination at the high priest's house, in which people are asked whether or not they know this man (Luke 22:54–60). No charges are brought against Jesus, no garments are rent, and no sentence or verdict of any kind is pronounced. This removes the presumption that Jesus should have been immediately taken out and stoned, thereby better defending the cruci-fiction story. On Friday morning, Jesus is given a short Jewish trial (Luke 22:66–71) before being handed over to Pilate.

The Roman trial in Luke 23:2–16 is most peculiar. In it, Pilate consults Herod the Tetrarch, since Pilate "knew that [Jesus] belonged under Herod's jurisdiction" (Luke 23:7). This would seem to have been inserted to meet the objection that if any ruler had final authority in the disposition of Jesus' sentence, it should have been Herod, not Pilate. But surprisingly, Herod and Pilate both agree that Jesus has done nothing wrong, and propose to release him (Luke 23:15–16). However, the crowd, whipped into a frenzy by the "chief priests," insists that Jesus be crucified, and Pilate is intimidated into complying. Of course, a crowd of Jews would not call for Jesus' crucifixion, but for him to be stoned. As if matters were not already confused enough, John 19:16 has Pilate handing over Jesus to the chief priests, so that *they* might crucify him!

Thus in Luke, the crucifixion of Jesus is more like a lynching than a judicial execution. One suspects that Luke's account having Jesus more or less lynched was composed to meet the objection that there was no conceivable legal procedure that could result in someone being crucified by the Romans for blaspheming the Jewish God. We recall that Acts 7 likewise depicts Stephen being lynched by members of the Sanhedrin, in a circumstance where his legal execution for blasphemy is in order. It is generally agreed that the author of Luke wrote at least some, if not all, of Acts. Here we detect the same hand at work in both manuscripts: both Jesus and Stephen are depicted as suffering extrajudicial execution by an angry mob, apparently to conceal the fact that the Sanhedrin was at that time still executing heretics by stoning them.

It is a well-known fact of New Testament scholarship that the degree of anti-Jewish sentiment increases with time.[36] Yet, in spite of this increasing hostility toward the Jews, the role attributed to the Jewish tribunal in condemning Jesus *decreases* uniformly from Mark to Matthew to Luke. This is the opposite of what one would expect, given other passages that betray a growing desire to portray the Jews in the worst possible light. This seems difficult, if not impossible, to explain, until we realize that the authors of the late Synoptics were carefully covering the tracks of any remaining evidence that might prove embarrassing to the cruci-fiction yarn. By shifting the judicial proceedings as much as possible from Jews to Romans, it softens the question that must undoubtedly have been raised: why was Jesus not stoned and hanged by the Jews for blasphemy, instead of allegedly being crucified? In all probability, the increasingly anti-Jewish tone of the later Synoptics was fueled by the Jews' unwelcome reminders about Jesus' illegitimate birth. However, the need to defend the cruci-fiction story by showing Jesus condemned and executed by Romans far outweighed the lost opportunity to make propaganda points against the Jews.

Did Jesus Die Too Soon?

The cruci-fiction story has always had a problem in that Jesus died much too soon. According to Mark, Jesus survived for six hours on the cross, from the third hour (after sunrise) to the ninth hour. The later Synoptics do not follow Mark in clearly specifying the duration of the cruci-fiction, probably in embarrassment at it being so short. John implies a shorter time still, having Jesus crucified sometime after the sixth hour (noon), with the time of his death not specified. Those whom the Romans actually crucified usually lingered on for several days in horrible agony. Thus we often hear the story of the Roman soldier's spear thrust into Jesus' side, to explain his unexpectedly sudden demise. However, John 19:34 plainly states that Jesus was *already* dead when the spear was stuck into him, still giving us no explanation of why he died so soon.

The later Synoptics omit all reference to Mark 15:44–45, in which Pontius Pilate expresses astonishment that Jesus should die so quickly. When Joseph of Arimathea requested Jesus' body, "Pilate marveled if he were already dead: and calling unto him the centurion, he asked him if he had been any while dead. And when he knew it of the centurion, he gave the body to Joseph." Out of 661 verses in Mark, 606—almost 92 percent—are found to be in Matthew, usually with only minor revision. Of the 55 Marcan verses missing from Matthew, 24 can be found in Luke.[37] Any of the 31 Marcan verses failing to make it into either of the later Synoptics, representing less than 5 percent of the total, is worthy of special scrutiny. Each contains what was later perceived as a problem in the earliest gospel. Probably recognizing that this passage called unnecessary attention to a problem in the cruci-fiction narrative, the authors of Matthew and Luke omit mentioning Pilate's surprise.

In certain ancient manuscripts of Matthew, just before Jesus "yielded up the ghost" in 27:50, we find appended to the previous verse, "and another took a spear and pierced his side, and there came out water and blood."[38] Most modern editions of the New Testament do not contain this passage, recognizing it as a later enhancement. This obvious defense of the cruci-fiction story must have been added to Matthew rather belatedly, intended to "solve" the problem of Jesus dying too soon.

Of course, if we accept the accounts of the Toldoth, of Acts, of Peter, and of Galatians, the difficulty immediately disappears. Jesus was already dead when his body was hung on the tree, and the body had to be taken down by sunset and buried on the same day, as commanded in Deuteronomy 21:22–23. Indeed, for the Jews hanging was not an approved means of execution—it was a means of displaying to the community the corpse of an executed offender.

When the Romans crucified someone, the victim was left on the cross for many days even after he was dead; indeed, the body was left hanging there until it decayed. As the putrefying body hung on the cross, the prey of vultures and other scavengers, it served as a very visible warning to others. In fact, it was forbidden for a victim of crucifixion to be taken down and properly buried. A soldier remained on duty next to the cross to ensure that no relatives or sympathizers would take the body down and bury it.[39]

A humorous illustration of this practice is provided by the *Satyricon* of Petronius, a picaresque first-century novel which gives us a remarkable glimpse of life in Nero's circle. In it there is a tale about a soldier assigned to guard the bodies of some thieves who had been crucified. During his nighttime vigil next to a graveyard, the soldier encounters a young woman in a nearby tomb mourning inconsolably over the body of her newly dead husband, refusing to eat or drink. He attempts to comfort her, gallantly offering to share his meals with her. One thing leads to another—the soldier is quite handsome—and soon he and the woman are enjoying one of the few heterosexual encounters in this exceedingly randy book. They spend three consecutive nights lost in each others' embraces.

One night, however, while the soldier is pleasurably occupied inside the closed vault, the parents of one of the crucified men quietly arrive. They take down their son's body from the cross—exactly what the soldier is supposed to be guarding against—and carry it off to give it a proper burial. When the soldier discovers the empty cross after sunrise, he is panic-stricken. Rather than wait for the magistrate to order his execution for dereliction of duty, he prepares to take his own life. But his paramour begs him not to, and she suggests another plan. Together they remove the body of her late husband from its tomb, and nail it to the empty cross. This apparently solves the difficulty.[40]

While the tale recounted by Petronius is fictional, it describes real practices of the mid-first century A.D. Victims hanging on crosses were expected to remain there as long as possible, as a gruesome warning to others. Soldiers were posted to ensure that nobody attempted to take them down. Yet in the cruci-fiction story about Jesus, we are expected to believe that soldiers watching the crucifixion were perfectly content to stand by as Jesus' followers took down the body, and gave it a hasty burial as sunset approached.

A later passage from Flavius Josephus' *Wars of the Jews*, written around the year 100, might seem to contradict Petronius. Josephus describes a time of fierce battles between Jewish religious fanatics and the Romans; during one slaughter perpetrated against civilians by a Jewish sect, "they proceeded to that degree of impiety, as to cast away their bodies without burial, although the Jews used to take so much care of the burial of men, that they took down those that were condemned and crucified, and buried them before the going down of the sun."[41] The meaning of this passage is not entirely clear. Josephus, referring to the behavior of Jews in more normal times before the war that resulted in the destruction of Jerusalem, implies that they took down and buried victims of crucifixion before sunset. But since those crucified would not normally die on the first day, it is not clear whether he means that they would be killed if necessary and taken down that same day, as John suggests happened with Jesus, or that on the day they did die, the body would be taken down and buried before sunset. Note, however, that Josephus says "condemned and crucified." Crucifixion may not have been the actual cause of death, for another passage in Josephus implies that crucifixion was normally, like hanging, inflicted on the corpse of one already executed. He remarks with apparent surprise that a Syrian king of the second century B.C. caused Jews to be "crucified while they were still alive and breathed."[42]

The prompt execution of the sentence of death, as well as the hasty removal and burial of the body, both strongly imply that Jesus' execution was carried out by Jewish authorities. But the Jews never executed offenders by crucifixion, and the Romans never hastened to take down and bury the bodies of crucifixion victims as sunset approached. Perhaps it was only permitted to remove bodies from crosses if the victim had already been dead when placed up there. The Romans forbade the burial of those they had crucified, while the Jews required burial of the bodies of those executed, before sunset, in a temporary burial site in a special cemetery, because executed persons could not immediately be buried in the community burial grounds. Eventually, when the bones were dry, they were removed and reburied with the others.

JESUS' BODY BECOMES A CURSE

The "cruci-fiction" story strikes us as a terribly confused account, a Roman execution carried out in strict observance of Jewish rabbinical law. Surely, it did not actually happen this way. Jesus must have been executed for blasphemy or heresy by the Jews, in the Jewish manner—by stoning, with the body hanging on a tree until sunset— as is plainly suggested in a number of ancient sources. The cruci-fiction account of Jesus' death must have been added perhaps twenty years later, when the Evangelists discovered how effective it was for inflaming proletarian resentments against the wealth and power of the Romans.

Paul gives us an extremely significant insight in Galatians 3:13: "Christ hath redeemed us from the curse of the [Mosaic] law, being made a curse for us: for it is written, Cursed is every one that hangeth on a tree." This is an obvious reference to Deuteronomy 21:22–23: "And if a man have committed a crime worthy of death, and he be to be put to death, and thou hang him on a tree: His body shall not remain all night upon the tree, but thou shalt in any wise bury him that day; (for he that is hanged is accursed of God;) that thy land not be defiled, which the LORD thy God giveth thee for an inheritance." This is precisely what the Toldoth says happened to Jesus; the statute in Deuteronomy was followed to the letter.

This remarkable passage in Galatians provides the strongest evidence of all that Jesus' body was literally hung on a tree, and not a cross. According to Paul, when the body of Jesus was hung on the tree, it became accursed, thereby taking onto itself the curse of the Mosaic law, which was now lifted from all who followed Jesus. There is *no* way that this passage in Galatians can be construed as referring to a cross, for there is nothing "written" in the Scriptures about curses accruing to bodies that hang on crosses. It *is*, however, very plainly "written" in Deuteronomy that curses became attached to the bodies of executed criminals hanging in trees, and this is obviously the passage to which Paul refers. Thus, it seems clear that Paul himself knew Jesus was not crucified, but hanged in a tree. This passage also shows that Paul viewed the Jewish law as a kind of "curse" from which he sought escape by any means, fair or foul. Here we see an extremely early and unsophisticated version of the later Christian doctrine that Christ took upon himself the sins of the world. Here we also see why Paul has been considered the "destroyer" of the Jewish law.[43]

The Gospel of Peter

The Gospel according to Peter was in widespread use in Christian worship from about 150 to 300. It was ultimately purged from the Canon, and lost for many centuries. However, an archaeological team uncovered a fragment of it during an excavation in Egypt in 1886.[44] In it, Herod is portrayed as the one giving the order for Jesus' execution, with a Jewish court apparently having found him guilty. It also depicts the Jews, not the Romans, handing over Jesus' body to Joseph of Arimathea. In this account, apparently "crucifixion" has become an option in Jewish law! There is nothing in it to suggest that Jewish courts lacked the authority to order executions. This gospel obviously attempts to deal with the objections that must have been raised to the cruci-fiction narrative, as described above. In it, Herod is portrayed as arranging, prior to the crucifixion, for Jesus' burial later that day, saying, "for it is written in the law, that the sun set not upon one that hath been put to death." This is an obvious reference to Deuteronomy 21:22–23, but the passage is very specific: *if* a man is put to death, in accordance with Jewish law, *and if* his body is hanged afterward, *then* it must be taken down and buried before sunset. There is nothing in this "law" that would apply to an execution carried out by Romans, nor is there any reason to believe that the Romans in Judea (or anywhere else) actually did take down crucified victims at sunset.

Another interesting feature in the Gospel of Peter is its obvious attempt to deal with the objection that victims of crucifixion should have been guarded by soldiers. A detailed account is given of the centurion and his soldiers who were supposedly assigned to guard Jesus' tomb, and of the miracles they are said to have witnessed there (such guards are also mentioned in Matthew 27:64–66). That the purpose of guarding the body is to prevent it from being buried does of course make the guards seem superfluous when the body is already interred, but it is better to guard the barn door after the horse has already fled than not to guard it at all. This gospel even tells us the name of the centurion said to be assigned this task: his name, remarkably, is Petronius.

The First "Epistle-General" of Peter

The first "Epistle-General" of Peter is of a very early date. If it was actually written by Peter, then it is earlier than about 64, the year of his death. (Of course, scholars cannot agree as to whether Peter actually wrote this. It seems that nothing can ever be agreed upon in the realm of New Testament scholarship!) In it, Peter claims to have been a witness to "the sufferings of Christ" (1 Peter 5:1), but he thinks Jesus' body was hung in a tree: "Who his own self bore our sins in his own body on the tree" (1 Peter 2:24). The authorship of the second "Epistle of Peter" is disputed by most scholars, on grounds of style and content. The reference to "the tree" in 1 Peter, and lack of mention of "the cross," would seem to suggest a very early date for the manuscript, as would its emphasis on the "last days." If Peter actually did write the first epistle that bears his name, then this passage is indeed a rock upon which we may build our proof that Jesus was hanged in a tree. No matter who wrote this epistle, its content is significant.

In The Acts of John, an early second-century "apocryphal" work, we likewise read that Jesus "was hung on Friday." This phrase likely reflects an extremely early tradition, before the cruci-fiction story was invented, or at least before it was firmly entrenched.[45]

The second-century "heretic" Marcion, whose influence for a time rivalled that of orthodoxy, apparently taught that Jesus had been hanged. Tertullian writes scornfully of "Marcion's Christ suspended on his gibbet."[46] A number of early "heretics," especially Gnostics, denied the reality of Jesus' crucifixion, on grounds that are somewhat unclear, and are traditionally interpreted as implying that a God cannot suffer and die. In many cases, our only knowledge of these "heretical" teachings is from their refutation by the orthodox.

Why Remove the Body?

Significantly, the Gospel of John gives us a completely different pre-text for the removal of Jesus' body: "The Jews therefore, because it was the [day of the Sabbath] preparation, that the bodies should not remain upon the cross on the Sabbath day, (for that Sabbath day was a high day), besought Pilate that their legs might be broken, and that they might be taken away" (John 19:31). Thus, according to John it would be perfectly acceptable for the victims to remain upon the cross all night, were it not for the approaching Sabbath which began at sundown Friday. Had the next day been some ordinary day, Jesus and the other victims could well have remained up there. The author of John does not seem to think that Deuteronomy requires the burial of crucifixion victims at sundown.

In Mark 16:1, three women brought "sweet spices" to Jesus' tomb, "that they might come and anoint him." Matthew deletes the reference to spices as well as to the women's intention, because he has invented soldiers supposedly "guarding" the tomb, to meet the objection that the bodies of crucified victims ought to be guarded after their death (even though the reason for guarding them was to prevent them from being taken down!). In Mark, there were no guards, hence the women thought it possible to anoint Jesus' body, although they belatedly realized that rolling back the huge stone might pose a problem. But since Matthew has invented soldiers to guard the tomb, he omits Mark's mention of the women's intention to anoint the body, because in this version they would know that there would be soldiers preventing anyone from entering the tomb.

DOES THE FICTION BEGIN WITH PAUL?

Judging by the evidence we have adduced, it is entirely reasonable to surmise that the cruci-fiction story was invented by Paul himself. He certainly invented enough *other* doctrines for the infant church! Significantly, Paul styled himself as "the apostle of the Gentiles" (Romans 11:13), and as such he had a clear interest in whatever doctrinal changes might make the new religion appeal more strongly to non-Jews. For promoting this aim, the cruci-fiction story was ideal. Resentment against the power of the Jewish hierarchy was limited to "the insurgents of Israel." But resentment against the power of Imperial Rome could be found everywhere, in every run-down hovel or every out-of-the-way street, in every city, town, and province of the Empire. Into such powder kegs the evangelists stealthily crept, fanning the flames of resentment against the educated and successful people of the Empire until those flames eventually erupted into a veritable firestorm.

The chronology of the New Testament Epistles is indeed significant. We must remember that there were no written gospels at the time of composition of the genuine Pauline Epistles, which contain few specifics about the life and teachings of Jesus; many of those details were filled in, or invented, later. It is generally believed that the earliest of Paul's Epistles, 1 Thessalonians, was written during his second evangelical journey, about the year 51. The "cross" or "crucifixion" is not mentioned in it. Galatians may have been written during Paul's third evangelical journey, which was about 54–58.* The Epistle of the Galatians is itself puzzling, because it mentions the cross numerous times, but it also refers explicitly to Jesus being hung in a tree. Perhaps later copyists altered the manuscript. Thus it would be reasonable to conclude, as a working hypothesis, that sometime around the year 55, Paul decided to alter the story of Jesus' execution from "hanged in a tree" to "crucified," because the revised story "sold" far better among the Gentiles. By this time, Jewish courts had for fifteen years been stripped of their authority to impose the death penalty. Presumably, Roman crucifixions were by then becoming common in Judea. In the absence of widespread written records, probably few people would know, or remember, that twenty-five years earlier—around the year 30, when Jesus was executed—Jewish courts still exercised that authority.

---

*Some scholars, however, believe Galatians to be the earliest epistle, while others place it after 1 Thessalonians.

By the time 1 Corinthians was written, "the cross" had become paramount in Paul's thinking. Indeed, it is possible to read the first two chapters of 1 Corinthians—an undoubtedly genuine letter of Paul—as a reply to those who objected to the newly fabricated story of Jesus having been crucified, pronouncing it foolishness. We find a singular emphasis on the crucifixion here as practically nowhere else, along with a spirited defense of foolishness. "Now I beseech ye, brethren, by the name of our Lord Jesus Christ, that ye all speak the same thing . . . there are contentions among you . . . Is Christ divided? Was Paul crucified for you? . . . For Christ sent me not to baptize, but to preach the gospel; not with wisdom of words, lest the cross of Christ should be made of none effect. For the preaching of the cross is to them that perish, foolishness. . . . But we preach Christ crucified, unto the Jews a stumblingblock, and unto the Greeks foolishness. . . . For I determined not to know anything among you, save Jesus Christ, and him crucified."

It is often said by New Testament scholars that Paul "theologized" the cross, in a way that Christianity's other founders did not. This suggests that the cruci-fiction story may have been his own invention. The cruci-fiction might be a "stumbling block" to the Jews for the simple reason that they knew it didn't happen. Admittedly, this inter-pretation is not the only one possible. Nonetheless, given that 1 Corin-thians, with its singular emphasis upon "the cross," was written very early in the history of the cruci-fiction story, it is tempting to see in this book Paul's attempts to rally an unruly congregation behind the new "party line."

During the third journey Paul is believed to have written epistles to the Corinthians and Romans. Both of these frequently mention the cross. The pseudo-Pauline epistles of 2 Thessalonians, Ephesians, and Hebrews are believed by most scholars to be later works by a different author. Such books were later "discovered" (i.e., fabricated) when it was found desirable to "clarify" Paul's views on certain subjects, such as the necessity for strict obedience to the church hierarchy.

THE LETTERS OF PONTIUS PILATE

The New Testament "apocrypha" contain several books and letters allegedly written by Pontius Pilate, who supposedly became a believer after witnessing the miracles that are said to have accompanied Jesus' execution. These are almost certainly forgeries perpetrated by Christian evangelists to bolster the faith. There are three accounts.[47] One of them is the very brief "Epistle of Pontius Pilate," allegedly written to the Roman emperor. In it, while "Pilate" claims that the Jewish "scribes, chiefs, and elders agreed to crucify this ambassador of truth" (an impossibility under Jewish law), he continues, "When he was hanged supernatural signs appeared." This is the shortest, and apparently the earliest, of three accounts of Jesus' death that Pilate supposedly sent to his emperor. While an obvious forgery, it is clearly a very old one, and we see that at this early stage Jesus was still "hanged," although a reference to the cruci-fiction is also in it. Later Christian writings seldom if ever refer to "hanging" or to "the tree."

The two later versions of this same bogus missive from Pilate reveal very clearly Christianity's process of "improving" its sacred writings to meet objections. The next such account was called "The Report of Pilate the Governor, Concerning Our Lord Jesus Christ, which was sent to Augustus Caesar in Rome." Immediately the perceptive reader will see a problem here; Augustus died in the year 14, nearly twenty years before the execution of Jesus. But Christian evangelists were noted for their faith, not for their worldy knowledge; nor, apparently, could truthfulness be counted among their virtues, when a forgery might prove effective. This supposed report has a second obvious problem. In it pseudo-Pilate describes the miracles that supposedly occurred while Jesus was on the cross (gone is any mention of "hanging"). He says that not only was the sun darkened for half a day, but the moon was dimmed, too, "as though tinged with blood." But Jesus was executed on the eve of Passover, and Passover always is celebrated at the time of the full moon. When the moon is full, the sun and moon are directly opposite each other in the sky. When one is above the horizon, the other is always below. Thus, it would have been impossible to see both at the same time, as pseudo-Pilate claims to have done.

Fortunately, yet a third report from Pontius Pilate to the emperor on this subject miraculously appeared in the ecclesiastical literature: "Th Report of Pontius Pilate, Governor of Judea, which was sent to Tiberius Caesar in Rome." It was nearly identical to the one that apparently preceded it. However, this time pseudo-Pilate got the name of his emperor correct. He also fixed the problem of claiming to see the sun and the full moon at the same time; now he says, "the moon, which was like blood, did not shine all night long." Thus the three synoptic epistles of pseudo-Pilate illustrate the process of altering "sacred" texts to meet objections, a process that has thus far baffled New Testament scholars; they are obsessed with finding so-called "hidden sources" to explain "the Synoptic Problem," when simple mendacity and forgery will suffice. The Church Fathers were extraordinarily fortunate in possessing so many correct and genuine, yet hidden, documents that could be pulled from their repository as soon as serious flaws were discovered in their predecessors.

THE TRIUMPH OF THE CROSS

One advantage to the cruci-fiction story, although distinctly a lesser one, is that it allowed Christians to claim Jesus' fate had been prophesied in Zechariah 12:10: "And I will pour upon the house of David, and upon the inhabitants of Jerusalem, the spirit of grace and supplications: and they shall look upon me whom they have pierced, and they shall mourn for him, as one mourneth for his only son." Remember that the Greek word that we see translated as "crucified" throughout the New Testament means literally "impaled." The early Christians made exensive use of this verse as an alleged prophecy of Jesus. Because Jesus' messianic credentials were exceedingly weak, his disciples needed all the prophetic assistance they could get. If they preached that Jesus was stoned and then "hanged on a tree," they could not claim Jesus as the fulfillment of Zechariah, because Jesus would not have been "pierced."

Upon a moment's reflection, it is obvious why it was in the evangelists' self-interest to change the story of Jesus' death from "hanged" to "crucified." The notion of a body hanging in a tree had a significant emotional impact only to those raised in the Jewish tradition, who were cognizant of the proclamation of Deuteronomy 21:23 that a body hung in a tree "is accursed of God." But the notion of a body nailed to a cross had a powerful emotional impact throughout the Roman Empire, for it was the Romans' favorite means of executing troublemakers from the lower strata. To be crucified was as much a symbol of shame as it was of suffering and death, because it was inflicted only on slaves and noncitizens. This severe punishment was inconsistently and often arbitrarily inflicted: one victim of crucifixion might have been a murderer, while another might have been guilty only of petty theft. There was undoubtedly a powerful undercurrent of resentment against the wealth, strength, and power of the Romans among slaves and others who were powerless, running throughout the length and breadth of the Empire. To these people, the cross was the very symbol of Roman power, a power not always magnanimous, and one that frequently was degraded to the level of brutality.

By claiming victory over the cross, Christianity rocketed into a position of power by harnessing this profound resentment directed against the Romans. As I noted in my earlier book, *Resentment Against Achievement*, the weak invariably harbor profound resentments against the powerful, even when the latter wield power sparingly and justly. Resentment is a consequence of weakness confronting strength, and not necessarily the abuse of strength. No doubt the earliest evangelists, attempting to preach the gospel of a prophet who was slain and hanged in a tree, found the story effective in rallying "the insurgents of Israel" (as they are called in the Toldoth). However, it evoked little or no response among the Gentiles, who cared not a bit how the Jews dealt with their insurgents, especially those of illegitimate birth. But make the claim that your prophet was nailed to a cross by the cruel Romans— as many people were—*yet that he vanquished the cross by rising from the dead*, and you will electrify the resentful throughout the far-flung Empire.

We might imagine it happening many times to the earliest evangelists that when they were preaching about Jesus, who was "slain," some listener asked, "you mean he was crucified?" And imagine the evangelists' dismay at finding, each time the question was truthfully answered in the negative, the Gentiles losing interest in the story, and moving on. Sooner or later, the temptation would become overwhelming to shout, "Yes! He was CRUCIFIED! And yet he has risen!" (Remember that there were no written records readily available, to which any interested person could refer. All information about the new religion, both pro and con, traveled by word of mouth.)

Whoever of the evangelists was the first to claim Jesus' cruci-fiction—whether the lie was calculated, or came in the heat of the moment—he was no doubt thrilled to see a wave of excitement sweep through his listeners as never before. It is unrealistic to expect these fanatical evangelists to let mere facts stand in the way of supremely effective rhetoric. They had a small problem in that some writings were already in regular liturgical use mentioning Jesus "hanging on the tree." These writings could not be suddenly or greatly altered, because the faithful had heard them many times, and no doubt many people had practically committed them to memory. But "the tree" could be explained as a convenient metaphor, and references to "the cross" could be put into new writings.

Perhaps surprisingly, the evangelists also must have found that the story of a crucified Messiah "sold" better among mainstream Jews as well, and not just to the resentful fringe of that group. Remember that Deuteronomy 21:23 proclaims that "he who is hanged [in a tree] is accursed of God." It would, of course, be an impossibility for pious Jews to accept anyone "accursed of God" as the true Messiah. Indeed, this is probably why the practice arose of hanging executed blasphemers and heretics, to prevent them from being revered or exalted after their death. For the Jews, hanging a body on a tree was the symbolic equivalent of driving a wooden stake through a vampire's heart, the symbol of an absolute and final end to a great evil. But if the claim is made that Jesus was crucified by the Romans, an enormous obstacle is removed against his status as "Messiah." While accepting a "crucified Messiah" might be difficult for Jews, a Messiah "hanged in a tree" was a complete impossibility.[48]

Thus we see that there are excellent reasons for believing that Jesus was executed for blasphemy or heresy by the Jews, in the Jewish manner. The cruci-fiction story was substituted later, when the evangelists discovered it far more effective in rallying "the insurgents among the Gentiles" to their cause. This was the first major fabrication of the Christian evangelists. As we shall see in succeeding chapters, it was not to be their last.

NOTES

1. G. A. Wells, *Did Jesus Exist?* (London, 1975); *The Historical Evidence for Jesus* (Buffalo, New York: Prometheus Books, 1988).

2. Eusebius, *Ecclesiastical History* 1:7, 3:20.

3. Gibbon says that the name of Athanasius "will never be separated from the Catholic doctrine of the Trinity, to whose defense he consecrated every moment and every faculty of his being." *Decline and Fall of the Roman Empire*, chapter XXI (New York: Modern Library Edition, n.d.), vol. 1, p. 698.

4. See I Infancy 19:22-24; I Infancy 20:14-16; II Infancy 2:1-16, of the New Testament Apocrypha, in *The Lost Books of the Bible* (New York: Bell Publishing Co., 1979).

5. James M. Robinson, *A New Quest of the Historical Jesus* (Philadelphia: Fortress Press, 1983), p. 178. This Strauss, against whose critical attacks on the Synoptics the Biblical literalists sought "liberation," is the same one whom the young Nietzsche inexplicably attacked in the first of his *Untimely Meditations*, "David Strauss, the Confessor and the Writer" (1873). He denounced Strauss as a "Philistine," an egomaniac, and a bad stylist. In

writing this, Nietzsche was clearly acting as a "hired gun" for the composer Richard Wagner, his early mentor, who was becoming increasingly pious in his old age (or at least pretending to do so). By this time Strauss had become quite highly regarded, and it seems that Wagner begrudged sharing the adulation of the German-speaking people with anyone else. The mature Nietzsche seems to have come full-circle, referring in *Antichrist* 28 to "the incomparable Strauss."

6. There is an excellent overview of these issues in the article "Gospels" by Bruce Manning Metzger in *Collier's Encyclopedia* (1978 ed.).

7. *The Interpreter's Bible* (New York: Abingdon Press, 1954), vol. 7, p. 645.

8. Frank Zimmerman, *The Aramaic Origin of the Four Gospels* (New York: Ktav Publishing House, 1979), p. 198. In arguing that the gospels (and indeed Acts and Revelation as well) were originally written in Aramaic (a view scholars generally reject), Frank Zimmerman suggests that the use of *xulon* can best be explained as a mistranslation of a certain ambiguous Aramaic word. But the rabbinical books, and many other sources, tell us that it was on a tree that Jesus was hanged, in accordance with Jewish law. In any event, few scholars accept Zimmerman's claim that most of the New Testament has been translated into Greek from original documents in Aramaic.

9. *Shorter Encyclopaedia of Islam*, H. A. R. Gibbs and J. H. Kramer, eds. (1953 ed.), s.v. "Isa."

10. Philip Carrington, *The Early Christian Church* (Cambridge: Cambridge University Press, 1957), pp. xiii–xiv. "The *Acts of the Apostles* comes to an end in the year 60, but many scholars think that it received its present form" after 70.

11. Evidence that the "fastened" passage from Peter's speech (Acts 2:23) is relatively old is given by the primitive Adoptionist view expressed nearby in Acts 2:36 (the "Adoptionist Heresy" is explained in the next chapter), a passage which nonetheless contains *stauroō*, "crucify." That Acts 5:30 is quite old is suggested by its primitive theology in proclaiming that "the God of our fathers raised up Jesus," implying that Jesus had not the power to raise himself, a view found throughout the genuine Pauline writings. Such views would be considered "theologically incorrect" by later writers of scripture. As for the date of composition of 1 Peter, it is estimated by *The Interpreter's Bible*, (vol. 12, p. 80) as approximately 63. Galatians is older still.

12. This passage does not appear in all early manuscripts of John, hence it was obviously a late addition; see *The Interpreter's Bible*, vol. 8, pp. 591–92. Also, the procedure described for the stoning is not in accordance with Jewish law; see the article "Capital Punishment" in *The Jewish Encyclopedia* (ca. 1905).

13. "An old-established rule of rabbinic jurisprudence forbids the in-

fliction of punishment where there is no Biblical authority for such punishment (Sanh. 82b)": see *The Jewish Encyclopedia*, s.v. "Capital Punishment."

14. In *Jesus Outside the Gospels* (Buffalo, N.Y.: Prometheus Books, 1984), pp. 8, 18, biblical scholar R. Joseph Hoffmann dates 1 Thessalonians from about the year 50, suggesting it to be the oldest book of the New Testament. Some scholars say that Galatians is the oldest, but clearly the two epistles are both extremely early, and very close in time.

15. Hiam Cohn, *The Trial and Death of Jesus* (New York: Ktav Publishing, 1977), p. 97. The author is a Justice of the Supreme Court of Israel.

16. See the article "Adultery" in *The Jewish Encyclopedia*.

17. Cohn, *The Trial and Death of Jesus*, p. 96.

18. Flavius Josephus, *Antiquities of the Jews*, Book XIV, 9:3–5.

19. Ibid.

20. See the article "Capital Punishment," *The Jewish Encyclopedia*; see Deuteronomy 13:1–10.

21. "Capital Punishment," *The Jewish Encyclopedia*.

22. R. Joseph Hoffmann, ed. and trans., Celsus, *On The True Doctrine* (New York: Oxford University Press, 1987), p. 130.

23. "ben Stada": see Hoffmann, *Jesus Outside the Gospels*, chapter 3. Hoffmann's Talmudic references are T. Sanh. X.11; J. Sanh. 7.16 (25c, d); b. Sanh. 43a. Avoidance of using Jesus' name: see "Jesus," *The Jewish Encyclopedia*.

24. One might surmise that the first telling of this story had Stephen executed for blasphemy by the Sanhedrin. But when it was realized what a problem this posed for the cruci-fiction story, the text was altered slightly to make it appear that the trial was halted, and Stephen was lynched. A comparison of Acts 7:57–58 with Luke 23:23 shows the same device employed in defense of the cruci-fiction story, probably by the same hand. Both use mob anger to "explain" an execution that would otherwise have no conceivable basis in law unless the Sanhedrin still retained the authority for capital punishment.

25. William Barclay, *Introduction to the First Three Gospels* (Philadelphia: The Westminster Press, 1975), p. 157.

26. Quoted by Eusebius, *Ecclesiastical History* 4:22.

27. Josephus, *Antiquities of the Jews* XX, 9:1; Origen refers to this passage in his *Commentary on Matthew* 10:17, and his *Contra Celsum* 1:13. Some dispute whether Josephus actually referred to James as the brother of Jesus, the "so-called Christ," but Josephus unquestionably recorded the stoning of James; "The Second Apocalypse of James"; an account of the "approved" method of stoning is given in the article "Capital Punishment" in *The Jewish Encyclopedia*.

28. See "Jesus," in the *Encyclopedia Judaica Jerusalem* (1971 ed.).

29. Hoffmann, *Jesus Outside the Gospels*, pp. 48–49.

30. *The Jerome Biblical Commentary* (Englewood Cliffs, N.J.: Prentice-Hall, 1968), vol. 2, pp. 57–58.

31. See the description of this ritual in Adam Clarke, *Clarke's Commentary* (Nashville: Abingdon, n.d.) on Acts 7:59.

32. Cohn, *The Trial and Death of Jesus*, p.114.

33. See the article "Cross, Finding of the Holy," in the *New Catholic Encyclopedia* (1967 ed.).

34. *The Jerome Biblical Commentary*, vol. 2, p. 58.

35. Ibid., p. 56.

36. "We see then that the anti-Jewish tendencies of the New Testament become more pronounced in the documents which scholars have regarded on other grounds as the later ones. And this is exactly what one would expect if these documents really are later and reflect the growing hostility of a new religion toward its parent." Wells, *The Historical Evidence for Jesus*, Section 4, part V.

37. Barclay, *Introduction to the First Three Gospels*, p. 86.

38. Burton H. Throckmorton, Jr., ed., *Gospel Parallels* (Nashville: Thomas Nelson Publishers, 1979), p. 183.

39. For crucified victims, "sepulture was therefore forbidden, and a soldier set to watch the corpse." *Harper's Dictionary of Classical Literature and Antiquities*, (1965 ed.), s.v. "Crux."

40. Petronius, *Satyricon*, sections 111–112. Federico Fellini's 1969 film version of the *Satyricon*, which is admitted to have been "freely" adapted from the Roman classic, depicts this scene. However, Fellini has for some reason changed the method of execution from crucifixion to hanging.

41. Josephus, *Wars of the Jews* IV, 5:2.

42. Josephus, *Antiquities of the Jews*, XII, 5:4. G. A. Wells likewise interprets this passage as implying that crucifixion (like hanging) was inflicted *after* execution (*Historical Evidence for Jesus*, chapter 1, part 7).

43. There is a long passage in Nietzsche on Paul as "the destroyer of the law": see *Die Morgenrote* (1881), section 68. (Translated as *Daybreak* by R. J. Hollingdale, Cambridge University Press, 1982). This passage also appears in Walter Kaufmann's *The Portable Nietzsche* (New York: Viking Press, 1968).

44. The Gospel According to Peter is included in *The Lost Books of the Bible* (New York: Bell Publishing, 1979).

45. Acts of John 97, in Ron Cameron, ed., *The Other Gospels* (Philadelphia: The Westminster Press, 1982), p. 94.

46. *Tertullianus Against Marcion*, "Pendentem in patibulo Christum Marcionis," 4:42. Many other passages plainly imply "hanging."

47. The forged reports attributed to Pilate were once in widespread use in Christian churches. All three are published in *Lost Books of the Bible*.

48. Of course, someone who doubts my "cruci-fiction" thesis might argue that the rabbinical authors invented the "stoning-fiction story" precisely *because* it would render Jesus ineligible as Messiah. But they then would face the challenge of showing how the "stoning-fiction" hypothesis better accounts for all the facts cited above than does my cruci-fiction thesis.

4

The Making of the Messiah, Part Two: The "Virgin Birth"

The second major fabrication of the Christian evangelists involves the claim of the "Virgin Birth." We recall from the first chapter the passage in which Tertullian waxes with excitement as he contemplates the "spectacle" of the coming day of vengeance, when he will look down on mighty emperors, governors, philosophers, and even Olympian deities groaning in unending torment in hell. As he savors the hierarchy inversion of this anticipated revenge, Tertullian saves up his greatest vindictiveness for a final epithet to shout at those writhing in agony below him: "This, I shall say, this is that carpenter's, or prostitute's, son, that Sabbath-breaker, that Samaritan and devil possessed!"[1] This same passage is quoted in Nietzsche's *Genealogy of Morals*, unfortunately only in its original Latin. When he gets to the Latin word meaning "prostitute" (*quaestuaria*), Nietzsche adds the comment in German, "this term for the mother of Jesus, which is found in the Talmud, shows that from here on Tertullian is referring to the Jews."[2] Pious Fathers and Reverends, the ones who seem to do most translations of books of this kind, have been known to mistranslate Tertullian's reference to the Jews' charge that Mary was a "prostitute," preferring to doctor the text of this ancient Church Father rather than open up old wounds which seem to them finally to have been closed for good.

Origen's third-century defense of Christianity, *Contra Celsum*, quotes Celsus' charge that Jesus "fabricated his birth from a virgin. He came from a Jewish village and from a poor country woman who earned her living by spinning. She was driven out by her husband, who was a carpenter for trade, as she was convicted of adultery. After she had been driven out by her husband and while she was wandering about in a disgraceful way she secretly gave birth to Jesus."[3] It is extremely unlikely that the "Virgin Birth" fable was invented by Jesus himself; indeed, nobody seems to have "known" this fact until Jesus had been dead at least fifty years. The blasphemous writings of Celsus have, of course, been hunted down and burned by Christians, surviving only in their refutation by Origen. The ecclesiastic historian Eusebius (approx. 263–339), like Origen, seeks to refute "those of the circumcision who slanderously and abusively assert that our Lord and Savior Jesus Christ was born of Panthera,"[4] which of course is what it says in the Toldoth.

There are numerous references in the Talmud to "Yeshua ben Panthera," literally, "Jesus, son of Panthera." This name is used quite matter-of-factly, as if everyone knew that Jesus the Nazarene was Panthera's son. While we cannot in our time say with certainty whether Jesus actually was the illegitimate son of Panthera, what we *can* be certain of is that the Jews of first and second-century Judea believed this, since we find it scattered throughout the rabbinical writings from that period.

Some have argued that "Panthera" is not actually a name, but a corruption of the Greek *parthenos*, meaning "virgin." Hence, Jesus was being called the son of a "virgin," not of a man named Panthera. But a first-century Roman tombstone now in the Bad Kreuznach Museum in Germany carries the inscription: "Tiberius Julius Abdes Pantera of Sidon, aged 62, a soldier of 40 years' service, of the 1st cohort of archers, lies here."[5] This may indeed be the tomb of Jesus' real father, or at least of a relative of his. Sidon is a very ancient seaport city in the Holy Land; Jesus is said to have passed through Sidon in Mark 7:31 (a detail unaccountably deleted by Matthew; the section has no parallel in Luke. Was Matthew just tightening up Mark's loose prose, or might a visit to what was probably the city of Panthera be embarrassing?). Origen argues against the view that Jesus was the illegitimate son of Panthera on the grounds that "the offspring of such impure intercourse must rather have been some stupid man who would harm men by teaching licentiousness, unrighteousness, and other evils," instead of righteous behavior. However, now that we know for certain that a parent's acquired characteristics are not transmitted through the genes, Origen's argument fails to convince.

In recent years, some liberal Christians have seemed willing to allow themselves to doubt the long-standing dogma of the Virgin Birth. What they apparently do not realize is that the moment they entertain the slightest doubt that the Holy Spirit created and shaped the appropriate strands of divine DNA inside Mary's body and miraculously fused them with the genetic data carried in her own chromosomes, they find themselves worshiping a bastard Messiah. It is very clear from Matthew 1:19 that when Joseph first noted Mary's pregnancy, he reacted not with self-confidence and delight, but with outrage. He obviously knew that the child was not his. This is abundantly confirmed by other sources, both Christian and Jewish. The mother of Jesus is therefore either a Holy Virgin, or else she is an adulteress; there is no third possibility.

A pregnancy in circumstances where one ought not to occur always poses a moral dilemma. Nonetheless, during the history of Christianity there have been a number of different solutions proposed to the problem of Jesus' paternity, other than the doctrine of supernatural conception. The Gnostic Christians generally did not accept the doctrine of the Virgin Birth. They tended to view Jesus as a purely spiritual being, a notion that seems to be suggested by John 1:14: "And the Word was made flesh, and dwelt among us." For example, one Gnostic text says that Jesus "was begotten in life, being in life because [body and soul] are in passion and changing opinion from the Logos [Word] who moved, who established them to be body and soul. . . . He came into being from the glorious vision and the unchanging thought from the Logos who had just returned to himself after his movement." In the fifteenth "secret saying" of the Gnostic Gospel of Thomas, Jesus implies that he should be worshiped because he was not "born of woman."[6] Since a spiritual being does not require an earthly mother or father, the problem of illegitimacy can in this way be solved. The second-century Gnostic and "heretic" Marcion promulgated a doctrine that solved Jesus' paternity problem splendidly. He taught that "Christ had appeared, suddenly, unannounced, and full-grown in the 15th year of Tiberius,"[7] which would have been 28 A.D. His one-time disciple Apelles taught an equally ingenious, although "heretical," answer to the paternity problem. Jesus, according to Apelles, "formed his body by taking portions of it from the substance of the universe," gathering together the appropriate elements according to their Aristotelian nature: hot and cold, moist and dry. After the Resurrection, Jesus no longer needed this body, and returned its elements to the world.[8]

THE ADOPTIONIST HERESY

Many early theologians taught that Jesus was in essence the "adopted son" of God. He was not born the Son of God, and did not become the Son of God until some specific later time. Jesus' "adoption" might have occurred at the time of his baptism, as Mark 1:11 seems to suggest, or it might have occurred later, at the time of the Resurrection, which seems to be suggested by Paul in Romans 1:3–4. This view was known to later theologians as the "Adoptionist Heresy." Heretical or not, the Adoptionist view of Jesus' relationship to the Father is clearly suggested by many early canonical writings, most especially by the opening chapter of Mark. Jesus simply appears upon the scene, just one among the many being baptized by John the Baptist. Jesus stepped into the river, and "straightaway coming up out of the water, he saw the heavens opened, and the Spirit like a dove descending upon him: And there came a voice from heaven, saying, Thou art mine beloved Son, in whom I am well pleased" (Mark 1:10–11). The Marcan account seems to suggest that these heavenly occurrences took Jesus by surprise. This earliest gospel, giving us no account of Jesus' birth or childhood, clearly seems to be implying that for some inscrutable divine reason, God simply adopted Jesus as his son at the moment Jesus was baptized. Mark 1:11 is an obvious allusion to Psalms 2:7, "Thou art my Son; this day have I begotten thee." This suggestion of Jesus being "begotten" as God's son this very day is explicit in the baptism scene of the now mostly lost second-century Gospel of the Ebionites.[9] Psalms 2:7 is quoted within a context of extremely primitive theology in Acts 13:33 to suggest Jesus' relation to the Father."[10]

JESUS BAPTIZED TO REMOVE
THE TAINT OF ILLEGITIMACY?

Few people realize that the very act of Jesus being baptized poses a thorny theological dilemma. Baptism, which had been practiced by the Jews long before the time of John the Baptist, was generally understood as a ritual for washing away sins. Thus, Adam and Eve were said to have stood for many days in a river up to their necks, doing penance for their transgression. *The Jewish Encyclopedia* cites the following passage to illustrate the traditional Jewish concept of baptism: "Wash your whole stature clean from impurity in running streams, and, with hands uplifted to heaven, ask for forgiveness for your doing: then the worship of God will heal gross impiety."[11] To a Jew, baptism might also symbolize purification and consecration, as well as expiation of sins. But Mark 1:4 plainly tells us that "John did baptize in the wilderness, and preach the baptism of repentance for the remission of sins." Therefore, the very act of Jesus seeking out baptism by John carries the strong implication that Jesus was troubled by some sins that he needed to remit. It suggests that whatever Jesus may have been doing in the period before his baptism would be better left unrecorded. Perhaps this is why we have been left no account of that period.

The author of Matthew, setting reed pen to papyrus in order to meet widespread objections being raised against Mark, is clearly aware of this implication. Thus he has John try to forbid Jesus from being baptized, as if to say, "You are not a sinner—what need have you of baptism?" But Jesus insists on going through with the ceremony anyway (Matthew 3:13–15). Mark, of course, made no mention about any reluctance on the part of the Baptist. Conversely, in the enigmatic and once authoritative "Gospel according to the Hebrews," now known only through a few surviving fragments, Jesus is pressured by his mother and brothers to submit to baptism by John, with Jesus at first refusing! They said to him, "John the Baptist baptizes for the forgiveness of sins; let us go and be baptized by him." But Jesus replied, "In what way have I sinned that I should go and be baptized?"[12]

By the time Luke was written, an even better solution to the problem had been devised. Luke 3:21 emphasizes that "all the people" were being baptized by John, and casually notes that Jesus was baptized as well. When Jesus' turn came, a voice from heaven interrupted the proceedings. This solution neatly removes any insinuation that Jesus had a tainted background. While Mark had suggested that "all the land of Judea" was being baptized, obviously that kind of statement, several verses before the mention of Jesus' baptism, did not suffice to avoid the appearance of a problem.

I would venture that the later Synoptic authors, having the benefit of the "Virgin Birth" tale, wished that the matter of Jesus' baptism had never even been brought up. But the author of Mark, assuming that everyone knew of Jesus' illegitimacy, *needed* to have Jesus baptized by John in order to make him pure enough to carry out a divine mission. The Gospel of John, which wants us to view Jesus as "the Word made flesh," has John the Baptist encountering Jesus, and even seeing "the Spirit descending from heaven like a dove, and it abode upon [Jesus]" (John 1:32). But it says nothing about Jesus being baptized. In that Gospel, the Baptist calls Jesus "the Lamb of God, which taketh away the sin of the world" (John 1:29), and implies that Jesus accomplished with the "Holy Ghost" the same thing that he, John, did with running water: taking away sins. Clearly the author of John did not approve of the idea of Jesus being baptized.

JESUS' EMERGING PATERNITY: HUMAN AND DIVINE

According to the *Ecclesiastical History* of Eusebius (2:15), the Gospel of Mark, accepted by scholars as the oldest gospel, was written after the death of Peter at the request of the Christians in Rome, who wanted to have in written form the life of Christ as preached by Peter. This statement is widely accepted. The death of Peter is believed to have occurred between the years 64–68, during the persecutions of Nero; thus Eusebius' statement accords quite well with the scholarly consensus that Mark was composed around the year 70.* By this time, the doctrine of the cruci-fiction had been firmly established; indeed, if Eusebius is to be believed,[13] Peter, about to be crucified, was by his own request crucified upside-down, since he proclaimed himself unworthy of dying in the same manner as Christ.

Remember that in this oldest gospel, we find no birth-story whatever concerning Jesus. He simply appears on the scene to be baptized. The changes in the Synoptic accounts can most parsimoniously be explained by the hypothesis that the author of Mark simply assumed everyone knew that Jesus was a bastard, and since the subject of Jesus' birth was an embarrassing one, the less said about it the better. The only passage in Mark to give us any indication of Jesus' earthly origins is Mark 6:3, "Is this not the carpenter, the son of Mary,

---

*Nonetheless, a few biblical scholars still dissent furiously over the accepted dates of all four canonical Gospels. Claude Tresmontant (*The Hebrew Christ* [Chicago: Franciscan Herald Press, 1989]), a Hebrew Scholar at the Sorbonne, insists that the Gospels were all originally composed in Hebrew: Matthew, and Luke in the late 30s, and Mark last of all between 50 and 60!

the brother of James. . . ." This passage tells us who Jesus' mother is, but gives us no hint about his father. It is the only passage in the oldest gospel to name Jesus' mother, a move that, like Jesus' being baptized, might later have been regretted by the authors of Matthew and Luke.

Discussing this passage, New Testament scholar R. H. Lightfoot observed that it was an insult to a Jewish man to call him the son of his mother; propriety and custom demanded that he be referred to as the son of his father.[14] Thus Mark 6:3 is actually a depiction of people insulting Jesus and his mother, effectively calling his paternity into question. The author of Matthew obviously longed to fix that problem, but since the Gospel of Mark was already in widespread use in the churches by the time he was writing, he did not want to risk too great a change to the familiar text. Thus the passage calling Jesus "the carpenter" was cleverly changed to call him "the carpenter's son" (Matthew 13:55), thereby softening the insult by referring to him first as the son of his father, then of his mother. By the time the Gospel of Luke was written, the sometimes embarrassing Mark had long fallen into disuse, so that Luke's author felt free to alter the passage much more freely, removing the insult completely: "Is this not Joseph's son?" (Luke 4:22).

In Mark, there is also a brief reference to an unstated but very serious problem, the prophecy that the true Messiah is supposed to be a son of the House of David, and to be born in Bethlehem, the city of David. Jesus of Nazareth, presumably a son of the House of Panthera, seems to be quite ineligible to claim to be the fulfillment of Messianic expectations. Thus, in Mark 12:35–37, Jesus calls the prophecy itself into question: "How say the scribes that Christ is the son of David?" He then launches into a resentful denunciation of the scribes' prestige and wealth. Here the author of Mark sought to establish that the Messiah need not come from the House of David, since Jesus so obviously did not. Clearly, if Jesus actually *was* descended from David, it would not have been necessary for him (or in any case, for the author of Mark) to question that expectation.

The Gospel of John, like that of Mark, lacks any birth narrative whatsoever. The author of John, like the author of Mark, must have assumed that everyone knew of Jesus' embarrassing illegitimacy, and hence said nothing directly about it. Nonetheless it intrudes into the text in several places. The Gospel of John pointedly avoids naming Mary as Jesus' mother, always referring to her obliquely as "the mother of Jesus," or some other evasive term. Even the Synoptic Gospels are somewhat reluctant about using her name. In the oldest Synoptic, Mary's name appears only once, in the passage insulting Jesus' paternity (Mark 6:3), and there in its Greek form, *Mari'a*. In the later Synoptics, Mary's name appears *only* in the birth fables, which may have been composed separately, the sole exception being the reflected image of Mark 6:3 in Matthew 13:55. The latest passage naming Mary in Luke is 2:34, and the latest nonreflective passage in Matthew is 2:11; both are part of the respective "infancy narratives." William Barclay notes that "Luke 3:1 reads as if it was intended as the beginning of a book." [15] That chapter begins, "Now in the fifteenth year of the reign of Tiberius Caesar, Pontius Pilate being governor of Judea, and Herod being tetrarch of Galilee, and his brother Philip tetrarch of Iturea and of the region of Trachonitis, and Lysanias the tetrarch of Abilene, and Annas and Caiaphas being the high priests, the word of God came unto John the son of Zacharias in the wilderness." Barclay continues: "This elaborate sixfold dating reads like the initial sentence of a book which proposed to relate certain historical events. It gives a fixed point in time for the start. There can be little doubt that Luke did originally mean for that sentence to be the opening sentence of his book. But as the gospel now stands there are two chapters before it." [16] If Luke originally began with what is now 3:1, then it did not disclose the name of Jesus' mother. The name of Jesus' mother was clearly an embarrassment to the writers of epistles and gospels, given the obvious lengths they go to avoid naming her.

The author of John was likewise aware of the thorny problem of Jesus' lack of a Davidic ancestry that his illegitimacy implies. John 7:40–43 says, "Many of the people, therefore, when they heard this saying, said, Of a truth this is the Prophet. Others said, This is the Christ. But some said, Shall Christ come out of Galilee? Hath not the Scripture said, That Christ cometh from the seed of David, and out of the town of Bethlehem, where David was? So there was a division among people because of him." In other words, many people were refusing to accept Jesus as the Messiah because he was born in Galilee, and not in Bethlehem which is in Judea, and because his ancestry was not Davidic. If Jesus actually *was* born in Bethlehem, and actually *was* of the House of David, he needed only to say so to clear up this misunderstanding. Yet he strangely did not. Since Jesus was presumably born in Nazareth, which is in Galilee, to make him fit Messianic prophecy it would be necessary to concoct a story having him born in Bethlehem, and to invent a genealogy showing him descended from David through an unbroken male line. The author of John either did not know the birth-stories fabricated in Matthew and in Luke, or, what is more likely, chose not to credit them if he did.

In John 8:19–40, Jesus discourses with a group of Jews, who ask him, "Where is thy father?" Jesus is evasive on the question. He explains that while the Jews are the descendants of Abraham, he is the son of "the Father." (If Jesus were the son of the Gentile Panthera, he would not be a part of God's covenant with Abraham, so he claims to have received divine instructions by a more direct route, inventing a perfect Divine Father to substitute for an illegitimate earthly one. The notion of Jesus as the "son of God" almost certainly had its origin in the ongoing disputes over his paternity, with much talk about "the father" and "the son.") The sons of Abraham, suggests Jesus, do the deeds of their father, while I do the deeds of mine. Their reply to him is wicked: "We be not born of fornication," clearly implying that *he* was (John 8:41). While the Greek term used, *porneia*, might possibly signify "fornication," it usually refers to "prostitution." The Jews tell Jesus that, unlike him, "we have one father." In this they may be chiding him for claiming two fathers, a legitimate one in Heaven to overshadow his illicit earthly one; more likely, and worse still, the remark would seem to mean that "the son of a harlot, not knowing his true father, may claim many putative ones."[17] In any case, an extremely grave charge against Jesus' mother is recorded in this gospel.

The primary context of the Gospel of John 7:40–8:59 is the problem of Jesus' illegitimacy. The section begins with a rather frank admission of Jesus' complete lack of Davidic credentials, and ends with Jesus being taunted for being "born of fornication," and pelted with stones. Between these two scenarios, some churchman later felt the need to insert a third that was not part of the original manuscript: Jesus imploring forgiveness for the woman taken in adultery (see chapter 3, note 12).

John 8:33–41 very strongly implies that Jesus was not even a descendant of Abraham, let alone of David. Panthera being a Gentile, a son of Panthera would not even be a full-blooded Jew. Clearly, these were potent arguments being used *against* Jesus' being the true Messiah. We see that the authors of Mark and John were truthful about Jesus' origins in that they simply avoided a painful subject, and hoped that the problem would eventually go away. To answer such objections, it was deemed necessary by the later Synoptics to "make" Jesus be born in Bethlehem, and to concoct a genealogy showing him descended from David.

Clearly, the guffaws over Jesus' illegitimate parentage did not die down as the author of Mark must have hoped, but apparently got worse. Hence, a second gospel was needed, one that offered "proof," to the faithful at least, that their miracle-worker not only was not a bastard, but was actually descended from the illustrious King David, and born in David's city. The Gospel of Matthew is believed to have been derived from Mark sometime between 75–100, probably around 80 or 85. It firmly asserts that Jesus was born in Bethlehem, from a virgin, although it is rather sensitive on that point, letting it slip out that Joseph doubted Mary's chastity and was planning to divorce her (Matthew 1:18–19, the only remaining passage in the orthodox Canon where doubts about Mary's chastity have not been purged). However, an angel is said to have come to Joseph in a dream to set his doubts to rest. Timid and pious translators, such as those of the King James Version, or Gideon's, make the passage imply that Joseph intended to keep Mary hidden from sight. The Revised Standard Version, more faithful to the Greek text, says that Joseph "resolved to divorce her quietly," although this would be an impossibility under Jewish law. A divorce would have to be a public, not a private, matter, and any accusations of infidelity had to be proclaimed openly.

DUBIOUS BIRTH STORIES AND GENEALOGIES

Matthew has now given Jesus two "fathers," an earthly foster father who gives him a link to the House of David, in addition to a heavenly Father, whose "spirit" miraculously caused Mary's pregnancy. Matthew for some reason gives us a genealogy of Jesus, from King David through Joseph, even while telling us that Joseph did not beget Jesus. This may be absurd, but it was necessary, since ancient Jews reckoned descent solely through the male line, and generally did not list women in their genealogies. For an example of what a proper genealogy is supposed to look like, see the First Book of Chronicles. No one would take seriously a genealogy of Jesus through Mary's ancestors.

There are still relatively few details in Matthew concerning Jesus' birth. No "birth in a manger," no shepherds keeping watch over their flock, or any of the other pious fabrications that have become in our minds synonymous with Christmas. Matthew 2:10–11 claims that the Star of Bethlehem hovered over the "house" where Jesus was born, which apparently was not a stable. In Matthew, Mary and

Joseph apparently lived in Bethlehem, and thus did not need to travel anywhere to have Jesus born in the city of David. Jesus' birthplace becomes Joseph's house in Bethlehem (Matthew 2:11).

Saint Ignatius, the Bishop of Antioch, who was martyred by wild beasts in the Roman ampitheatre around 107, is the earliest Christian authority to state the doctrine of the Virgin Birth. No doubt he had been greatly vexed by impious tongues wagging about Jesus' illegitimacy. It was during his lifetime that the Gospel of Matthew was written, and it is not unreasonable to surmise that the good bishop may have had a hand in inserting the "Virgin Birth" fable into it, since that fable appears to have been his own invention. This suspicion is strengthened by the fact that a number of New Testament scholars believe the Gospel of Matthew to have been written in Antioch.[18] As I noted before, biblical scholars tell us that Matthew was derived from Mark by adding new material from a source called Q. The problem is, nobody really knows what Q was; like the famous x of algebra, Q is simply a name applied to an unknown. Fortunately for the young Christian faith, Q contained precisely what was needed to counter embarrassing charges from the impious that the Christian "Messiah" was born of fornication.[19] Interestingly, in some early manuscripts Matthew 1:16 proclaims Joseph the actual father of Jesus, not merely the husband of Mary. There are no fewer than four different wordings of Matthew 1:16 in different early manuscripts, which is highly unusual, indicating that the exact relationship between Joseph, Mary, and "the Christ" must at one time have been extremely controversial.[20]

Luke's Birth Fable

Luke, the latest of the Synoptic Gospels, was probably written around the year 100. By the time Luke was written, the fable of the Virgin Birth had flowered into wondrous detail; the more time having passed since the event, the more was known about it, a miraculous reversal of the process of entropy that normally degrades information and knowledge of past events. Like the author of Matthew, the author of Luke dipped into the miraculous Q, this time fishing even deeper, and seems to have discovered the biggest pile of Q ever. Once again, Q contained precisely what was needed to silence impious tongues that were merrily wagging about the unchastity of Jesus' mother.

In Luke we have the charming Christmas story, the decree of Caesar Augustus that everyone in the Empire must be taxed, the birth in the stable because "there was no room for them in the inn," the angel appearing to the shepherds "keeping watch over their flock by night," and so on. The birth-story in Luke is so charming that one almost feels guilty of slandering a mythology worthy of Homer or Ovid when reason compels one to note that the chances of this late addendum to the gospels being grounded in fact are virtually nil. This yarn, tender and charming though it may be, was inserted into Luke to attempt to silence, once and for all, the charge that Jesus was the bastard child of a woman who had been driven out of her home when her betrothed discovered her pregnant. It was enormously successful.

Luke, like Matthew, gives us a genealogy of the "generations of Jesus." However, the remarkable thing about these two genealogies is that they disagree. Matthew shows Joseph being descended from King David in twenty-seven generations, while Luke shows the same descent, through different names, in forty-one generations. Even the name of Joseph's father is different in each! Presumably God must have become seriously confused while inspiring the scribes of these infallible texts; either that, or serious objections were raised to the genealogy in Matthew, requiring a new one to be invented. One obvious objection to the genealogy in Matthew is that, since King David lived a thousand years before Jesus, twenty-seven generations—an average of thirty-seven years each—was an unrealistically small number in a society where girls were routinely married off at age fourteen. Forty-one generations—an average of twenty-four years each—is far more credible.

Disreputable Women in Jesus' Genealogy

There is, however, an even greater objection that was undoubtedly raised. The Jewish Encyclopedia notes that the genealogy in Matthew places "singular emphasis upon sinners and heathen ancestresses of the house of David."[21] Only the male image is traced through all the way, which is how Jewish genealogies had to be reckoned, yet four female ancestors of Jesus are nonetheless named in the Matthean genealogy. All four of them, significantly, are women of ill repute. Tamar, Jesus' ancestress according to Matthew 1:3, became "with child by whoredom" (Genesis 38:24). Rahab (or "Rachab"), Jesus' ancestress by Matthew 1:5, was a "harlot" of Jericho (Joshua 2:1). Ruth, also proclaimed Jesus' ancestress in Matthew 1:5, lay down with Boaz at midnight, when he was drunk (Ruth 3:7-14). Jesus' female link to the House of David is proclaimed in Matthew 1:6 to have been Bathsheba ("she that had been the wife of Urias"), who committed adultery with King David (2 Samuel 11:2–5). At the end of this unflattering genealogy we find yet one more woman's name—Mary.

Jesus' Disgraceful Male Ancestors

These fallen women are not the only objectional characters found in the Matthean genealogy. Of Josias (a.k.a. Josia, Joachim, or Jehoiakim), king of Judah, Jesus' ancestor according to Matthew 1:11, God says in Jeremiah 36:30–31, "He shall have none to sit upon the throne of David: and his dead body shall be cast out in the day to the heat, and in the night to the frost. And I will punish him and his seed and his servants for their iniquity." Another ancestor claimed for Jesus was Jechonias (Coniah), the son of Josias according to Matthew 1:11 although actually his grandson according to 1 Chronicles 3:15–17. He fares no better. God decrees for Jechonias' fate, "Write ye this man childless, a man that shall not prosper in his days: for no man of his seed shall prosper, sitting upon the throne of David, and ruling any more in Judah" (Jeremiah 22:30). Looking carefully at the genealogy in Matthew, it is obvious that someone with encyclopedic knowledge of the Scriptures has gone to great pains to select the most objectionable names possible as Jesus' ancestors.

When this genealogy proclaiming Jesus to be descended from the most notorious disinherited kings and fallen women of the Old Testament was read off with pride in the Christian churches, it no doubt resulted in many new impious horselaughs among the Jews. It probably did not take the church long to realize that it had been "had" by whomever it entrusted to make up this genealogy. A new and more respectable genealogy was quickly drawn up and attributed it to the Apostle Luke. In Luke the references to harlots and the disinherited have been carefully removed; gone are mention of Tamar, Ruth, and Rahab. (Being David's ancestresses, they implicitly are still there, but their names are no longer called out.) Gone completely are the embarrassing Bathsheba, Josias, and Jechonias. Jesus' Davidic link is now traced through David's son Nathan, born before David had been tainted by adultery, and bearing the same name as the respected prophet who later chastised David for that great sin.

One cannot help but conclude that the author of Matthew must have asked a Jewish scholar for assistance in preparing the genealogy of Jesus. No matter how long that rabbi may have lived afterward, I doubt if he ever stopped laughing about this trick. Christianity is not the only major religion to have been duped into enshrining a Jewish joke in its Holy Scripture; a similar trick seems to have been played upon Muhammad. The name of Jesus in the Koran is "Isa," which many scholars trace to the Jewish practice of scornfully calling Jesus "Esau," after the Old Testament figure who "despised his birthright." Apparently Muhammad received some of his information about Jesus from Jewish sources, and failed fully to investigate opposing views.[22]

The Pauline Account

In the genuine Pauline Epistles (probably 1 Thessalonians, Romans, 1 and 2 Corinthians, and Galatians),[23] as in the nonderivative Gospels of Mark and John, Jesus is implicitly a bastard. In Romans 1:3–4 Paul sets forth an Adoptionist position, that Jesus became the Son of God upon his Resurrection. Paul was, of course, writing thirty or forty years before Ignatius' remarkable "discovery" that Jesus had been born from a virgin; nobody living decades earlier, nobody who had actually *known* Jesus, seems to have been aware of that astonishing fact.

Paul tells us nothing about Jesus' mother or father. G. A. Wells writes that "the few facts Paul does record about Jesus' incarnate life—his descent from David, the reproaches to which he was subjected, and his death (in unspecified circumstances)—are all said to be 'according to the Scriptures.' " In other words, these are things that must be so not because they are historical fact, but because such was the prophecy. Wells further notes that when Paul "goes on to detail the humiliation and persecution he has suffered as a Christian, he tells them [Christians] to 'be imitators of me' (1 Corinthians 4:11–13 and 16). When he later repeats this injunction, he makes the claim that he himself is an 'imitator of Christ' (11:1), as if implying that Christ lived a life of humiliation (cf. 1 Thess. 1:6). . . . Christians did not, in Paul's day, have to reckon with being killed for being Christians. . . . Paul's statement, then, is that 'we' Christians share [Jesus'] sufferings, but since this cannot mean his crucifixion, it refers to the fact that his life was one of suffering."[24] Now, if Jesus was a "humble carpenter," as Christians have suggested, this is absolutely no cause for "suffering" or "humiliation." Even a "humble carpenter" would be respected by his neighbors if he was honest, and obeyed all the religious laws. But the son of an adulteress would be an outcast, an object of great opprobrium, precisely matching Jesus' life as suggested by Paul.

Birth Stories in the Apocrypha

The "apocryphal" Gospel of the Birth of Mary was used in worship in many ancient Christian churches. Scholars disagree as to its source and date. By some accounts, it was in widespread use by the fourth century, and was accepted by St. Jerome and many of his contemporaries. Others claim this is bogus, judging it to be a seventh-century work, but one nonetheless derived from earlier sources.[25] This book ceaselessly proclaims the virginity of Mary, telling how she spent her youth as a temple-virgin, devoted to the service of the Lord, who held daily conversations with angels and other visitors from God. At age fourteen, she was betrothed to Joseph, of the House of David, "a person very far advanced in years" (Mary 6:1). At that time, she was visited by an angel, who told her she would miraculously conceive a child. (Much trouble could have been avoided had the angel delivered that message to Joseph at the same time.) She did not see Joseph again until three months after the betrothal, at which time her pregnancy could not be hidden from him. (In actuality, a pregnancy of three months is usually not obvious.) He immediately became "uneasy and doubtful." Being a just man, he was unwilling to denounce her, "nor defame her by the suspicion of being a whore," so he decided "privately to put her away" (Mary 8:5-7). But then an angel of the Lord appeared to him in his sleep, and said, "Be not willing to entertain any suspicion of the Virgin's being guilty of fornication," explaining that the child was actually the Son of God. The book closes with Joseph taking his wife to his home city of Bethlehem, where she gives birth.

Note how these passages largely agree with the birth fable in Matthew. In these two gospels, Joseph lives in Bethlehem. (If Joseph did live in Bethlehem, one cannot envision any "respectable" reason why his wife would be compelled to give birth in a stable in that city; that she apparently did suggests that he actually did drive her out.) This apocryphal gospel has traditionally been attributed to St. Matthew.[26] Were it not for the suggestion of a late date of composition for this book, it would seem that the Gospel of Mary was written as part of the same damage-repair effort that created the Gospel of Matthew, but was dropped from the Canon when it was found not to be needed. In any case, the Gospel of Mary appears to contain a more primitive version of the story told in the Protevangelion of James (see below), which the *New Catholic Encyclopedia* dates to around the year 150. The birth yarn in the Gospel of Mary, like that in Matthew, says nothing about any empire-wide tax census necessitating travel.

Another "apocryphal" book, the Protevangelion of James, was widely accepted by the early Church Fathers. It tells the same story as the Gospel of Mary, in more detail, and appears to have solved some problems in the other work. The birth fable in the Protevangelion contains a number of distinctly Luke-ish elements, such as the tax decree of Augustus, which nicely solves the problem of why a respectable woman might give birth in a stable—an especially troublesome problem should that stable be in the same town where her husband lives, as it is according to Matthew and the Gospel of Mary. This account also contains elements from Matthew's birth-fable, such as the coming of the Three Wise Men and the Star of Bethlehem. The Protevangelion must have been composed after Matthew and Luke had been written, probably in an attempt to reconcile the two incompatible birth-fables. This book has the birth of Jesus taking place in "a cave" (some accounts have it in a stable in a cave); Origen says that this cave was still being shown in Bethlehem in his day.[27] In the Protevangelion's strange conflation of the two canonical birth-fables, Mary, learning of the impending Massacre of the Innocents, wraps the infant Jesus in swaddling clothes and hides him in the hay of an ox-manger. The Protevangelion also contains a number of otherwise-unknown miracles attending Jesus' birth, such as birds of the air being frozen in mid-flight, with the general appearance of time having stopped for everyone but the Holy Family.

In this book, we find once again the assertion that Joseph was an old man, who had been miraculously selected by God to betroth (but apparently to never have sex with) the virgin. Joseph objected at first, saying, "I am an old man, and have children, but she is young, and I fear lest I should appear ridiculous in Israel" (Prot. James 8:13). However, Joseph finally complied, then left Mary behind while he went off for six months to build houses. When he returned, he "found the virgin grown big." (Note how the problem of "the virgin grown big" at three months has been fixed; she is here given six months for her belly to swell.) Joseph was horror-stricken, and wondered what to do: "Is not the history of Adam exactly accomplished in me? For in the very instant of his glory, the serpent came and found Eve alone, and seduced her" (Prot. James 10:5–61). Mary maintained her innocence, strangely claiming that she did not know what the pregnancy meant. (Had she forgotten what the angel had told her?) Joseph decided to turn her out quietly, but then an angel appeared to him to proclaim her innocence.

However, their problems were not yet over. Annas the scribe visited Joseph, and perceived "the virgin big with child." He immediately denounced them both before the priests, who summoned them to the temple. Joseph was implausibly charged with having "defiled the Virgin whom he received out of the temple of the Lord, and hath privately married her," the first and only Jew ever to face such absurd charges. Joseph then underwent the ordeal of "the water of the Lord, which is for trial," for those accused of adultery (see Numbers 5:18). Fortunately, it established his innocence and thereby saved Mary the indignity of having to undergo the ordeal herself.

Such a public accusation and ordeal involving Joseph and Mary may well have taken place—but it could not possibly have occurred as described above. For under Jewish law, the crime of adultery was always charged against the *woman*, not against the man. This is made abundantly clear in Numbers 5:12–31, and is directly stated in the article "Adultery" in *The Jewish Encyclopedia*. Under this law, the one compelled to undergo the public ordeal and drink "the water of the Lord" would have been Mary, not Joseph. What would have occurred—and probably did, since the Talmud calls Mary a "known" adulteress—is that Joseph, finding Mary pregnant by someone else, publicly accused her of adultery. The law on adultery made no distinction between betrothed and married women.

The Jewish law against adultery was very strict. Everyone knows the account in John 8:3–11 of an adulteress about to be stoned. However, stoning as a penalty for adulteresses seems to have been only rarely imposed, and in any case New Testament scholars recognize that passage in John as a late addition. In actuality, stoning was only imposed as a last resort against a woman who had been repeatedly warned against adultery, and also warned about a particular man, but who carried out a liaison with him nonetheless. In nearly every case, the punishment facing an adulteress would be immediate divorce and public humiliation. Jewish courts only rarely imposed death sentences, for offenses they considered extremely grave. Evidence of mitigating circumstances was invariably sought.

If Mary had been so accused, she would have been brought before the Sanhedrin. Had she admitted the charges, she would have been divorced at once. Had she denied them, she would have been taken to the East Gate of the Temple, where a priest would perform the ceremony described in Numbers 5. Dressed in black, she would have had her garment rent, exposing her breast to the jeers of onlookers. A rope would then be tied around her chest as though she were an animal. A "jealousy offering" that was essentially animal gruel would be placed on the altar, to signify the beastly nature of the alleged offense. She would be made to drink water from an earthen vessel into which dust from the Temple floor had been mixed. She would be told that Yahweh would make these waters rot her guts out if she were guilty and did not confess.[28] This obviously constituted an extremely potent form of intimidation, and we can imagine that there were few women in this situation who did not confess, whether guilty or not. Even if the woman did not confess, her husband could still divorce her if he wanted to. Therefore, if Mary, while pregnant, had been driven out from Joseph's household in this manner, a public outcast, it would explain why she had to give birth in a stable, and not in a house.

The Jewish Encyclopedia cites Talmudic references that Mary (actually "Miriam"), the mother of Jesus, was "known" to be an adulteress. It states, "It is certain, in any case, that the rabbinical sources also [like Celsus] regard Jesus as 'the son of Panthera' . . . (Mary) was known to be an adulteress."[29] In order for this to be "known," as opposed to merely "conjectured" or "believed," it would seem that, at minimum, a public accusation of adultery must have been made against her. In all probability, she confessed to the charge—given how intimidating were the proceedings against accused adulteresses—and she would then have been publicly driven out by her betrothed. This appears to have been common knowledge among Jews at that time, given the sheer number of references to Mary's putative lack of chastity in the early Christian writings, and in the contemporary Jewish ones as well. Hence the mangled yarn having Joseph, not Mary, successfully passing the ordeal for adultery must have been put into the Protevangelion of James to allow Christians to interpret that shameful event in a more favorable light.

In all probability, the Gospel of Mary and the Protevangelion of James, while written to answer the charges of Mary's fornication, were ultimately removed from the Canon because they were not needed for that purpose. The accounts in Matthew and Luke sufficed to persuade Christians that Mary was "perpetually virginal"—and in any case the gospels about Mary were far too emphatic in denying her chastity problem, which served only to call more attention to it. Probably the "sanitized" version of the ordeal for adultery was inserted in the Protevangelion to provide a version of that painful and apparently widely known incident that the faithful could contemplate without too much alarm. No doubt anyone critically reviewing this account soon would have raised the objection that it should have been Mary, not Joseph, who had to submit to "the water of the Lord." But for the Holy Virgin to undergo such an ordeal would be unthinkable for a pious Christian even to contemplate.

The incorporation of the "water of the Lord" incident into Scripture constitutes an admission by the Christian leadership that some such public accusation of adultery had indeed been made. But life in ancient Jewish society was tightly regulated by "the Law," i.e., the first five books of Scripture. Lawbook and prayerbook were one. If Mary and Joseph were involved in a trial by "the water of the Lord," it must have taken place exactly as described in Numbers 5:12–31, since Jewish authorities did not tolerate the slightest deviation from what they believed to be God's commands. This embarrassing ordeal provided yet another motivation to later shield the gospels about Mary from public view. We also learn from these two non-canonical gospels that a girl of fourteen was betrothed to a man well along in years, who appears to have been a widower, and who was absent for long periods of time. Human nature being what it is, such a domestic situation (should that description in fact be accurate) practically seems to have been chosen to maximize the possibility that adultery would occur.

The Gospel of Nicodemus

The apocryphal Gospel of Nicodemus (also known as the "Acts of Pilate")[30] was once also widely used in Christian worship. It, too, was probably dropped from the Canon, not because it was any less "authentic" than books that remained, but because it discussed too freely the disputes which then raged concerning the legitimacy of Jesus' birth. This book contains a lengthy account of the supposed trial of Jesus before Pilate. In it, one group of Jews says, "We know this concerning thee: that thou wast born through fornication" (Nicodemus 2:7). This was countered by another group of Jews: "We cannot say he was born through fornication; but we know that his mother Mary was betrothed to Joseph, and so he was not born through fornication." (That Joseph knew the child not to be his, as is clear from Matthew 1:19, is conveniently not mentioned.) "Then Pilate said to the Jews who affirmed him to be born through fornication, This your account is not true, seeing there was a betrothment, as they testify who are of your own nation. Annas and Caiaphas spake to Pilate, All this multitude of people is to be regarded, who cry out, that he was born through fornication, and is a conjuror; but they who deny him to be born through fornication, are his proselytes and disciples" (Nicodemus 2:8–10). Finally, Pilate "commanded every one to go out except the twelve men who said he was not born through fornication," so they could be questioned. (In other words, all the Jews present except the twelve disciples said Jesus was born through fornication.) It is obvious why the Gospel of Nicodemus had to be deleted from the Canon; the sheer number of accusations and denials of "fornication" concerning the Holy Virgin was enough to drive a saint to drink. Also, Jesus' disciples, who should have replied that Jesus was born of a virgin to be doctrinally correct, said instead that he was the natural son of Joseph.

JESUS' BIRTH IN A STABLE

Another element in the story of the birth of Jesus not addressed by Matthew, but given a respectable explanation in Luke, is Mary's giving birth in a stable and not in her home, as one might expect. Apparently it must have been well known among the earliest Christians, and the Jews as well, that Mary had been on the move during her final days of pregnancy, and had given birth to Jesus in some ignoble place like a stable or a cave (or a stable inside a cave). This is, to say the least, an extremely unusual situation, even for the presumed wife of a humble carpenter. In fact, Celsus charges that Joseph had driven Mary out of his home when he found her to be pregnant by someone else, which is exactly what he threatens to do in Matthew and in the Protevangelion of James, and clearly would have done except for angelic intervention. As Mary was wandering about, a fallen woman in disgrace, she presumably sought refuge in a stable, where she delivered, in great shame, loneliness, and suffering, her illegitimate child. Why we say Jesus was born in a "manger" is perplexing. Luke 2:16 says that Jesus was lying in a manger, not that he was born there. A "manger" is simply the feed-trough used for livestock; indeed this English word is identical in spelling to the French verb "to eat." The baby Jesus may well have rested in the hay of a manger, but his birth occurred in a stable. Nonetheless, we repeatedly find references to Jesus' "birth in a manger," instead of in a "stable." Luther's Cradle Hymn should properly be sung, "Away in a stable, no crib for his head." This choice of words no doubt reflects our later, more refined sensitivities on such matters. We know that a "stable" is a dirty, smelly place, full of flies and feces. Ind ed, given the standards ʋf sanitation prevailing two thousand years ago, we can expect stables of that time to have been much filthier than those we know today.

Luke, however, saves Mary's reputation by inventing a respectable reason for a properly married woman to give birth in a stable. Caesar Augustus is said to have ordered that "all the world be taxed" (Luke 2:1), a remarkable decree apparently requiring everyone in the Empire, even if old or infirm, or in the final days of pregnancy, to get up and travel somewhere to be counted and taxed. It should not be the least surprising that "there was no room at the inn" if the entire Roman Empire was indeed required to uproot itself at the same time and go off somewhere to pay taxes.

Unfortunately for the credibility of Luke, this astonishing proclamation of Augustus was totally unknown to the historians who routinely chronicled the most minute details of Roman political life, and seems also to have been unknown to the Christians as well until they wrote this birth fable. One would expect that the sheer chaos caused by such a decree, requiring perhaps the largest mass-movement of people in history, would have made it a well-remembered event. Ian Wilson, after examining the principal historical sources concerning the alleged decree of Augustus, concludes, "to put it bluntly, Luke has resorted to invention."[31]

The supposed "Massacre of the Innocents," part of the birth fable in Matthew, is another dramatic event associated with Jesus' nativity that is likewise unknown to historians.[32] Thus Matthew apparently also felt the need to resort to a colossal historical falsehood to motivate Mary, Joseph, and the baby Jesus to leave their home. One would suppose that if there were some innocent reason for Mary and the infant Jesus to flee their home, Matthew and Luke would have found no need for such large-scale mendacity.

Equally dubious is the description of Augustus' supposed decree in the Protevangelion of James 17:1, in which it is said that the emperor merely decreed that "all that were in Bethlehem of Judea should be recorded." This supposed decree is also mentioned in the "apocryphal" First Gospel of the Infancy of Jesus Christ. That such a trivial decree would be issued by an all-powerful emperor is highly doubtful. Given that we see from the gospels that Judea was literally crawling with Rome's tax collectors, called "publicans," such a decree seems scarcely to have been necessary. Surely these publicans must have been equal to the task of counting and taxing the inhabitants of Bethlehem, or any other town. If such decrees were indeed issued from time to time for obscure little towns, history has not recorded them. What *is* clear, however, is that Christian writers were desperately grasping for some explanation to allow Mary to give birth in a stable, and spend the infancy of Jesus wandering about, without having been driven out as an adulteress. Given the sheer implausibility of Augustus' actually issuing any decrees of this kind, or Herod the Great's massacre of the children without historians noting, Celsus' explanation of Mary's wanderings seems by far the most credible.

In the description of the birth of Jesus in the Koran (Surah 19:16–34), Mary "withdrew" by herself to "a far place" after being visited by the spirit of Allah in the form of "a perfect man." She took refuge under the trunk of a palm tree, giving birth to Jesus in great isolation, pain, and despair. "Oh, would that I had died ere this!" she exclaimed. Allah, however, nourished her by providing a stream from which to drink, and he arranged for ripe dates to fall from the tree upon her. When she presented the child "to her own folk," their comment—apparently directed to her, although clearly more appropriate to the child—was, "Thy father was not a wicked man, nor was thy mother a harlot." The infant Jesus then miraculously speaks, explaining that he is a prophet of Allah. Surah 4:156 accuses the Jews of "speaking against Mary a tremendous calumny."

JESUS THE *MAMZER*, NOT THE SON OF GOD

The knowledge of Jesus' illegitimate birth is reflected in the Gnostic as well as in the orthodox writings. For example, the Gnostic Gospel of Thomas, lost for many centuries until its fortunate discovery among the Nag Hammadi texts in 1945, contains 114 "secret sayings of Jesus." "Secret saying" 105 is: "Jesus said, 'He who knows the father and the mother shall be called the son of a harlot.' " To understand the meaning of this, we must recall that in Gnostic theology, God is androgynous, not merely a Father but Father and Mother in one. Thus, Jesus is actually saying, "Anyone who knows the deity will be called the son of a harlot—that explains why you hear this said about me." Given the many passages written by Jews and other unbelievers in which Mary is depicted as an "adulteress" or worse, there can be little doubt as to the meaning of this passage.[33]

We now begin to understand why Jesus was treated as such an outcast in Jewish society, and why his open defiance of "the powers that be" gained him such an ardent following. *The Jewish Encyclopedia* states, "The child of an incestuous or adulterous connection was known as a *mamzer*. It was not permitted to become a member of the Jewish body politic [Deuteronomy 23:2], and could not intermarry with a Jew or Jewess."[34] While *mamzer* translates into English as "bastard," the Hebrew word is a much harsher one, and is used in a more restricted sense. While "bastard" describes the offspring of parents who are not married, *mamzer* refers to the child of parents who *could not possibly become married*: adultery or incest is clearly implied. If a man and woman who were not married conceived a child, strong social pressures dictated that they would become married; their child would then be recognized as fully legitimate. Jewish law was exceedingly harsh on the *mamzer*, who found himself despised and an outcast in every way, beyond any possibility of remedy. Deuteronomy 23:2 thunders, "A bastard [*mamzer*] shall not enter into the congregation of the LORD; even to his tenth generation shall he not enter into the congregation of the LORD." This is a powerful curse indeed, and as "the revealed word of the Lord," it was followed to the letter by ancient Jewish society.

In Mark 6:3, the passage that insults Jesus' paternity, we find that when Jesus was preaching in the synagogue, the people were "offended" by him. Christians usually interpret this passage to mean that the people were offended when a humble carpenter dared to preach in the temple. Unbelievers take it to suggest how inane and simplistic Jesus' message was. But we now see a more direct and powerful explanation: the people were offended because a bastard had entered into the Congregation of the Lord. Indeed, he had even dared to preach there! Here we discern yet another tacit admission in Mark of the illegitimacy of Jesus' birth. In the corresponding passage in Matthew (13:57), the people are still "offended in him"; presumably the author of Matthew, having softened the insult to Jesus' paternity a few lines earlier, did not realize what the "offended in him" was tacitly admitting. But by the time we get to Luke, it was realized that having people take offense at Jesus in the temple conceded his illegitimacy—clearly the most embarrassing problem Christianity faced at the time—and hence the passage was altered so the people no longer "were offended" but instead "wondered at the gracious words which proceeded out of his mouth," even though they became "filled with wrath" at his message (Luke 4:22, 28).

Clearly, the main goal in writing the birth fable in the Gospel of Luke, the final Synoptic, was to put to rest forever the problem of Jesus' illegitimacy. In this it was exceedingly successful. Thus we find in Luke—and *only* in Luke—passages written to convince us that Jesus did indeed "enter into the Congregation of the Lord," and hence could not possibly have been a *mamzer*. Luke 2:21—and no other passage—tells us that Jesus was circumcised in the Jewish manner. (A rabbi would presumably not circumcise a *mamzer* baby. John 8:33–41 strongly implies that Jesus is not "Abraham's seed," i.e., that he is uncircumcised.) Luke 2:22-27—and no other passage—has the infant Jesus properly presented in the temple at Jerusalem. We read in Luke 2:41-47—and nowhere else—of Jesus going to Jerusalem with Mary and Joseph for the Passover at age twelve, and how his discourse there amazed the learned scholars. If these purported events are true, and were known to the earliest Christian chroniclers, it is surprising that they did not record them, and if they were not known to the early chroniclers, it is puzzling how the later ones discovered them. The motivation for inventing such passages in the final Synoptic Gospel is transparently obvious: to convince the world that the young Jesus most certainly did take part in Jewish religious rites, and hence could not possibly have been a *mamzer*.

Being a *mamzer*, Jesus was the object of general opprobrium, owing to a situation over which he had no control. As outcasts, bastards naturally gravitate to the politics of *ressentiment*. Shakespeare understood this clearly; see his treatment of it in the role of Edmund, bastard son of the Earl of Gloucester, in *King Lear*. In our own time we see *mamzer*-anger expressed in the political careers of Fidel Castro and Manuel Noriega.[35]

For centuries, Christians have assumed from the fact that Jesus never married, and had no known involvement with women, that his Godly nature precluded all interest in the opposite sex. Now we see a more direct explanation: as a *mamzer*, Jesus was forbidden to marry any Jewish woman. Indeed, his status was very much like that of the Indian "untouchable," his very presence being most unwelcome in "respectable" circles. According to some interpretations, Jesus' only close female friend or associate seems to have been Mary Magdalene, who is generally represented as a former prostitute, now reformed. The "heretical" Gnostic Christians wrote that "the companion of The Savior is Mary Magdalene. Christ loved her more than all the disciples and used to kiss her often on her mouth."[36] This suggests a Jesus who was more fully human than the unworldly figure whom the orthodox worship.

THE CONFUSED IDENTITY OF MARY

Jesus' kissing Mary Magdalene, while it might make him appear more human, is historically doubtful. First, the work cited above, the Gospel of Philip, which is the source of this account, is judged to be a late third-century work. This is some 250 years after Jesus lived, affording ample time for legend and invention to work their way into the narrative. Second, there are excellent reasons for doubting that any "Mary Magdalene" ever existed. R. Joseph Hoffmann notes that when the Jews referred to Jesus' mother (Miriam in Hebrew) as the "dresser of women's hair" (for this was said to be her occupation), the Hebrew phrase is *Miriam, m'qadella nashaia.*[37] Thus the earliest Christians, and would-be Christians, heard much from Jews about *Miriam m'qadella*, who was said to be a prostitute. They were talking, of course, about Jesus' mother. It is likely that Christian propagandists, realizing that such talk was not about to go away, invented a new character, whose *name*—not occupation—was *Miriam m'qadella*, and who was indeed once a prostitute. That way it could be claimed that all the terrible things being said about *Miriam m'qadella* referred to this other, once disreputable woman, and not about Jesus' mother.

We find in the gospels yet another confusing "Mary," "Mary the mother of James and Joses" (Mark 15:40, 15:47, 16:11; reflected in Matthew 27:56, 27:61, 28:1; Luke 24:10). Similar circumstances suggest that she may be the same as the "Mary the wife of Cleophas" in John 19:25, said to be the sister of the mother of Jesus, whom John refused to name. Given that this Mary's two sons happen to match, both in name and in order of birth, Jesus' siblings as enumerated in the paternity insult of Mark 6:3, it is difficult not to infer that this Mary and Jesus' mother might be the same. One might surmise that these other Maries were fabricated to attract whatever invective might otherwise be directed toward the mother of Jesus.

DID JESUS HAVE A MALE LOVER?

While we can rule out a romantic dalliance between Jesus and Mary Magdalene, we have at least some grounds for believing that he followed the common Hellenic practice of erotic involvement with young men. Dr. Morton Smith, Emeritus Professor of Ancient History at Columbia University, made a remarkable find in 1958 in the ancient Middle Eastern monastery of Mar Saba. Dr. Smith found what is apparently the sole surviving copy of a long-lost letter of the second-century Church Father, Clement of Alexandria. In this letter, Clement refers to a "secret" version of the Gospel of Mark containing passages that do not appear in the canonical version.

The supposed "missing passages" seem to answer a number of long-standing puzzles about this earliest gospel. For example, there is a strange gap at Mark 10:46, where Jesus is said to have gone to Jericho and immediately to have departed from there. If Jesus did not go to Jericho for any reason, and did nothing significant there, why even mention the journey? (Matthew 20:29 and Luke 18:35 settled the problem of an apparently pointless trip to Jericho by deleting mention of the "coming and going.") According to Clement's letter, the deleted passage covering Jesus' stay in Jericho says: "And the sister of the youth whom Jesus loved and his mother and Salome were there, and Jesus did not receive them." [38]

Those who reject the idea of "secret" portions of the Gospel of Mark as revealed in Clement's new-found letter should ponder the words of Clement himself in an undisputed work, The Instructor: "The Mysteries of the Faith not to be Divulged to All. . . . Since this tradition is not published alone for him who perceives the magnificence of the word, it is requisite, therefore, to hide in a mystery the wisdom spoken, which the son of God taught . . . it is difficult to exhibit the really pure and transparent words respecting the true light, to swinish and untrained hearers." [39] Elsewhere Clement wrote, "Not grudgingly did the Lord declare in a certain gospel, 'My secret is for me and the sons of my house.' " [40] Scholars have long pondered why Hippolytus (ca. 170-236) refers to Mark as "stunted" or "maimed." Some suppose this to refer to a physical deformity of the author himself, but the term has also been interpreted as applying to the Gospel text. William Barclay [41] suggests that the Gospel of Mark is "maimed" because it has "lost its original ending" and therefore recounts no post-Resurrection sightings of Jesus. While it remains conjectural that any such "original ending" ever existed, Morton

Smith's finding gives us a far better reason for calling the Gospel of Mark "stunted" or "maimed": portions of it have been censored from the authorized version.

Another apparently excised Marcan passage uncovered by Professor Smith represents an earlier version of the story of the raising of Lazarus that otherwise appears only in John. It raises a difficulty, however, in that it has Jesus and Lazarus spending a night together in a circumstance suggestive of homosexual love. Clement, in his letter, explicitly denies rumors that were apparently going around erotically linking Jesus and Lazarus. Clement's letter helps explain why the author of John, writing perhaps thirty or forty years after Mark, refers to Lazarus as "he whom (Jesus) lovest" (John 11:3) but is careful to add that "Jesus loved Martha, and her sister, and Lazarus" (John 11:5). Thus John 11:5 clearly shows its author to be sensitive to the question of the manner in which Jesus "loved" Lazarus. A note in *The Anchor Bible* suggests that John 11:5 was a "parenthetical insertion," one which presents a paradox with the verse immediately following it. It is suggested that the motivation for its insertion was to assure the reader that Jesus' failure to go to Lazarus does not reflect indifference.[42] But a more likely reason is to diffuse the proclamation of Jesus' "love" for Lazarus in 11:3 to extend to Martha and her sister as well.

We find in John frequent but puzzling references to "the disciple Jesus loved." All such passages occur after Jesus' raising of Lazarus. "It has often been argued from Johannine evidence that the unnamed 'Beloved Disciple' was Lazarus."[43] In John 13:23 we find this puzzling male disciple "leaning on Jesus' bosom." Christians, horrified at the hint of homoerotic behavior in their Savior, explain this away as the traditional oriental posture of leaning on a couch during a banquet. However, the text very plainly states that Jesus rose from his dinner, changed his clothes, washed the feet of his disciples, and only then settled back, cradling the head of the Beloved Disciple. Also, there seems to be a very clear textual difference between merely "lying (or leaning) back" at a table (as in Matthew 9:10, Luke 22:14, John 6:11, etc.), and the disciple actually lying on Jesus' bosom or chest (John 13:23; 13:25). Many people "lean back" at tables in the gospels, but the Beloved Disciple is the only one who ever lies on anyone's "chest" or "bosom."

In John 19:26–27, Jesus' last act before expiring is to direct the disciple "whom he loved" to become the adopted son of his own mother; his last concern is apparently to bind together his lover and his mother. We note that when Lazarus was supposed to have died, "Jesus wept" (John 11:35). This is the only individual in the gospels whose misfortune brings Jesus to tears. "Then said the Jews, Behold how he loved him!" (John 11:36)

Of course, other identifications for "the Beloved Disciple" have been suggested, all of them less scandalous than the above. Many accept the suggestion in John 21:24 that the "Beloved Disciple" is none other than the author of that gospel, John himself. But this chapter is known as "the Epilogue" of John, regarded by scholars as a later addition by a different hand. Hence the identification has little credibility, since this chapter was, like other sacred addenda, written to *meet objections*. That it was felt necessary to identify "the Beloved Disciple" in a later problem-solving chapter gives credibility to Morton Smith's interpretation: clearly, *something* seemed improper.

These passages in John powerfully suggest that Jesus' "love" for the Beloved Disciple was more Socratic than Platonic. We must remember that homosexuality was acceptable behavior throughout the Greek world, but not to Jews. If Jesus did go and live in the Hellenic world after being rejected by the Jews because of his illegitimate birth, then there was nothing either surprising or shameful in his taking a young male lover, except in the eyes of the Jews.

A further suggestion of a Hellenized Jesus is Origen's comment that Jesus was "a great wrestler."[44] The sport of wrestling was very popular among the Greeks, but it was scorned by pious Jews as a "heathen game." Wrestling, like all other sports, was performed naked (hence, *gymnasium*, a place for naked exercise). This would make visible the mark of circumcision that distinguished Jew from Gentile. Jews who participated in Greek sports were made to feel ashamed of their visible sign of God's covenant with Abraham, and hence naked exercise was deemed inappropriate for pious Jewish men.[45] Indeed, the Dead Sea Scrolls proclaim that any man who goes naked before his companion must do penance for six months.[46] The great German poet Heinrich Heine frequently asserted that humanity could be divided by its worldview into "Nazarenes" (by which he meant Christians or Jews) and "Hellenes," and nothing more clearly illustrated the difference between the two than their reaction to nudity.[47] Thus, if Jesus became skilled in wrestling, a type of naked exercise, he did not learn that skill from Jews. It would not have been difficult for the young Jesus to encounter Greeks. While Nazareth was entirely Jewish, it was "little more than a suburb" of Sepphoris, the largest city of the region outside Jerusalem, a city "Greek in culture and language."[48]

The hidden passages of Mark also seem to explain another Marcan puzzle concerning the youth in the garden who fled at the time of Jesus' arrest. "And a young man followed [Jesus], with nothing but a linen cloth about his body; and they seized him, but he left the linen cloth and ran away naked" (Mark 14:51–52, Revised Standard Version). Here is another of the rare Marcan passages that did not find its way into either Matthew or Luke, signaling that there is something objectionable about it. Yet on the surface nothing appears to be wrong. However, if this boy was "the youth whom Jesus loved" from the censored part of Mark—probably the same as "the disciple Jesus loved" in John—that would explain why the later Synoptics eliminate all mention of him. It might also explain why the authorities tried to arrest this youth when they arrested Jesus, although they did not attempt to apprehend Peter or any other of Jesus' disciples. If we assume that "the youth whom Jesus loved" was named Lazarus, then the attempted arrest of the "youth who fled in the garden" in Mark is immediately explained by John 12:10: "the chief priests consulted that they might put Lazarus also to death." Apparently orders went out to arrest Jesus and Lazarus.

CONCLUSION

Rational persons have long shaken their heads in dismay to think that anyone would shed blood, as the early Christians did, over such seemingly vacuous matters as whether or not Jesus existed with the Father "before all worlds" or how many "persons" there are in the Godhead. The famous "Arian heresy" hinged on whether Jesus was of the "same substance" or of "like substance" as the Father. In Greek, the two words differ by a single letter—iota—hence the commonplace saying about things that do not even differ by "one iota." Gibbon wrote, "The profane of every age have derided the furious contests which the difference of a single diphthong excited between the Homoousians and the Homoiousians."[49]

These disputes have long been interpreted as bizarre manifestations of a pathological fanaticism. Yet when we understand the delicate issues raised by the problem of Jesus' paternity, we can discern a foolish consistency in the insistence on these doctrines; they follow directly from the defense of the Virgin Birth fable. For example, one of the arguments "Against Heresies" by Irenaeus is stated as follows: "The Apostles teach that it was neither Christ nor the Savior, but the Holy Spirit, who did descend upon Jesus."[50] Why should anyone care?

If we keep our terminology straight, we can readily understand the problem Irenaeus and the other orthodox theologians faced. Some were teaching that before Jesus' baptism, he was nobody in particular. Jesus was *literally* just some poor bastard who wandered into the right place at the right time when The Father needed a certain task to be performed. In this view, "The Christ" or "The Savior" was a divine person, or at least a divine role, that happened to descend upon Jesus of Nazareth when he was baptized; it might as easily have descended upon someone else. The account in Mark of Jesus' baptism seems to support this view. All of Jesus' previous sins were wiped away by John's baptism, at which time this new divine mission descended upon him like a mantle, immediately eradicating the stigma of his illegitimate birth.

Defenders of the Virgin Birth fable needed to establish that Jesus of Nazareth was *already* an extremely significant person at the time of his baptism, indeed at the time of his birth, in order to refute decisively the "Adoptionist heresy." Therefore, they needed to argue that Jesus was not just some poor bastard who happened by, but was instead "begotten by the Father before all worlds, true God from True God." Yet there still remains a problem. Plainly, *something* from Heaven must have descended upon Jesus at the time of his baptism. If it was not the mantle of The Anointed One—if Jesus was born carrying that—what could it have been? Thus, a *third* Divine Person was needed in the Godhead, separate from the Father, who speaks from Heaven, and from The Christ, who is standing on earth. This matter was deemed important enough to spill blood over, for if Jesus was nobody in particular until his baptism, then it would not be believed that his mother could have given birth and remained a virgin. What is left, then, is Jesus the bastard son of Panthera, hobbling the growth of a new religion.

We must be careful to understand that Jesus was not in any way opposing Roman rule—the kind of action that might get him crucified—or the worship of the Greco-Roman gods, including the emperor. His attack was directed exclusively against Jewish religious rules and customs: the Sabbath, the dietary restrictions, and other requirements of "the law." Jesus ceaselessly proclaimed to the Jews that the laws of Moses were now superseded by the laws of *his* father— a being who must be presumed to be in Heaven since no trace of him can be found on earth.

One cannot help but sympathize, however, with Jesus, who suffered so greatly from the persecution under "the law" owing to his illegitimate birth, through no fault of his own. One can readily imagine the bitter resentment that he must have felt against that hated, harsh, inflexible law. Indeed, it would be most amazing if no *mamzer* had ever openly challenged "the law." Perhaps others did. But as these others were not alleged to have risen from their tomb, their names are lost to history. At the same time, one must try to understand the Jewish religious authorities who, viewing themselves as the custodians of their people's unique covenant with the One True God, were so angered by Jesus' undermining of their rules that they condemned him to be slain and hanged on a tree.

When Jesus rose up in open rebellion against the religious and secular authority of the Jews—and let us remember that there existed at that time no separation of church and state—everyone who held a grudge against "the powers that be" was electrified by him. It matters little whether those grievances had any degree of legitimacy or not. People at the bottom of society were delighted to see someone with the courage to do what they had always secretly longed to do: rise up against those considered upright and just. Whether their problems were of their own making, the consequence of laziness, mendacity, and envy, or were caused by factors beyond their control—such as their parents' want of chastity—they vicariously enjoyed Jesus' triumphs as if they were their own. The resentful were delighted by his audacity. Just as the child in class who stands up to the teacher and loudly refuses to do the assignments is watched by the other children who all wish secretly to do the same, waiting to see what punishment he meets, the scum and dross of Jewish society gleefully followed Jesus around, eager to see how far he might get in his open rebellion against the Law and the Prophets. When Jesus was arrested, slain, and hanged on a tree, it seemed as if the fun was over. The rule of law seemed to have been restored. But on the third day, "the insurgents of Israel" were set on fire by the news that Jesus allegedly had risen from the dead—a claim we will examine in detail in the next chapter.

Twentieth-century sociologists talk about the "Big Lie" as if it were the shocking invention of modern totalitarians. A "Big Lie" occurs when one opposes an unpleasant reality with a lie so utterly bold that its very magnitude seems to compel belief. A small lie, one that merely denies an unpleasant reality, is often not sufficient to compel belief; world-class liars feel that a charge against them must not merely be denied, but stood on its head by vehemently asserting the strongest possible claim to the contrary. Thus the professional liars of the ██████████ claimed that they did not ██████████, but instead had ██████████ just in time from a ██████████ to destroy it. Similarly, their Soviet counterparts lied that the Berlin Wall was put up not to prevent escape, but to "protect" East Germans from Western spies and saboteurs.

But our twentieth century wrongly fancies itself the inventor of "The Big Lie"; the technique far predates us. The "makeover" that transformed the bastard son of Panthera into a glorious, high-born king from the House of David surely required no small degree of mendacity. And what else can we call it if not a "Big Lie" when the fanatical founders of a totalitarian religious order fabricate new "holy books" in order to transform a woman with a reputation for unchastity into one who is "perpetually virginal"?

NOTES

1. Tertullian, De Spectaculis 30. " 'Hic est ille,' dicam, 'fabri aut quaesturiae filius, sabbati destructor, Samarites et daemonium habens.' "

2. Nietzsche, Genealogy of Morals, First Essay, Section 15. See the translation of the rest of this passage from Tertullian, and Kaufmann's comments on it, in Walter Kaufmann, Basic Writings of Nietzsche (New York: Modern Library, 1968), pp. 485–86. The fanaticism of this passage is also commented on by Gibbon in chapter XV of The Decline and Fall of the Roman Empire (New York: Modern Library, n.d.), vol. 1, p. 406.

3. Origen, Contra Celsum 1:28.

4. Eusebius, Ecl. Proph. 3: 10, quoted by Henry Chadwick in his notes to Origen's Contra Celsum (Cambridge University Press, 1980), p. 31.

5. There is a photograph of Panthera's tombstone in Ian Wilson's Jesus, The Evidence (San Francisco: Harper & Row, 1984).

6. The quote about "the Logos" is from The Tripartite Tractate, a newly discovered document. See The Nag Hammadi Library in English (New York: Harper & Row, 1981) I, 5: 115, 14. The Gospel of Thomas is likewise part of the Nag Hammadi Library (II, 2: 35, 27).

7. New Catholic Encyclopedia (1967 ed.), s.v. "Marcion."

8. Hippolytus, Refutation of All Heresies 7:26.

9. Burton H. Throckmorton, Jr., ed., Gospel Parallels (Nashville, Tenn.: Thomas Nelson Publishers, 1979), p. 11.

10. Note how primitive is the theology suggested by Acts 13:29–34. Jesus was hanged on a tree. After his death, he was raised up by God.

(Note the use of the passive voice several times; apparently Jesus had not the power to raise himself.) It is suggested that Jesus was "begotten" as God's son on the day of his Resurrection. These passages undoubtedly were written very early, probably around the year 60; they cannot possibly come from the author of the sophisticated Gospel of Luke.

11. See the article "Baptism" in *The Jewish Encyclopedia* (ca. 1905), s.v. "Baptism." The quote is from Sybyllines IV:164 et seq., quoted in the article "Circumcision."

12. From a fragment of Hebrews quoted by Jerome in *Against Pelagius* 3:2, In Throckmorton, *Gospel Parallels*, p. 10.

13. Eusebius, *Ecclesiastical History* 3:1.

14. R. H. Lightfoot, *History and Interpretation in the Gospels* (New York, 1934; quoted in *The Jerome Biblical Commentary* [Englewood Cliffs, N.J.: Prentice-Hall, 1968]), vol. II, p. 33.

15. William Barclay, *Introduction to the First Three Gospels* (Atlanta, Ga.: John Knox, 1976), p. 201.

16. Ibid.

17. Clement of Alexandria, *Exhortation to the Heathen*. Its context is that of a general statement and is not applied to Jesus.

18. See "Ignatius of Antioch," in the *New Columbia Encyclopedia* (1975 ed.). B. H. Streeter, in *The Four Gospels* (New York: The Macmillan Company, 1925), is among those scholars placing the composition of the Gospel of Matthew in Antioch; of course, some other scholars offer differing views. See *The Interpreter's Bible* (New York: Abingdon Press, 1951), vol. 7, p. 241.

19. I am not attempting categorically to deny that there has ever existed some sort of collection of "sayings of Jesus" that has come to be known as Q. Indeed, the early Gospel of Thomas in the recently discovered Nag Hammadi Library suggests that there may have been. However, the scholarship of the past century has revealed that even many of the "sayings" of Jesus are dependent upon pre-Christian material, or are otherwise of highly questionable authenticity (see the discussion in chapter 2 of William Barclay, *Introduction to the First Three Gospels* [Philadelphia: The Westminster Press, 1975]). This casts further doubt on the existence of some mysterious Q as an independent, generally reliable source of "new" information about Jesus and his "sayings." In general, it is a mistake to imagine that the non-Marcan additions to Matthew and Luke—especially obvious responses to problems, such as the birth stories—were added because new information "became available."

20. Throckmorton, *Gospel Parallels*, p. 2.

21. *The Jewish Encyclopedia*, s.v. "Jesus."

22. *Shorter Encyclopaedia of Islam*, H. A. R. Gibb and J. H. Kramer, eds. (1953 ed.), s.v. "Isa."

23. R. Joseph Hoffmann suggests that these are the only letters "coming more or less directly" from Paul. See *Jesus Outside the Gospels* (Buffalo, N.Y.: Prometheus Books, 1984), p. 130.

24. G. A.Wells, *The Historical Evidence for Jesus* (Buffalo, N.Y.: Prometheus Books, 1988), pp. 35–36.

. 25. The introduction to this work in *The Lost Books of the Bible* (New York: Bell Publishing Company, 1979), suggests an early date for this book, while the *New Catholic Encyclopedia*—which in describing the book does not dare to hint at the chastity problem it raises—says that the gospel was written around the year 800 (see the article "Bible III: Apocrypha of the New Testament"). Yet it seems unlikely that any book calling great attention to Mary's problematic pregnancy would be composed at such a late date, when the "problem" of Jesus' paternity, as well as those of the New Testament Canon, had both long since been set to rest.

26. See the introduction to this work in *The Lost Books of the Bible*, p. 17.

27. Origen, *Contra Celsum* 1:51.

28. *The Jewish Encyclopedia*, s.v. "Adultery."

29. *The Jewish Encyclopedia*, s.v. "Jesus." The Talmudic references are to Shab. 104b; Sanh. 67a.

30. The "Gospel of Nicodemus," part of the New Testament Apocrypha, is included in *Lost Books of the Bible*.

31. Wilson, *Jesus, The Evidence*, p. 55. In a footnote, Wilson writes, "For a definitive appraisal of the Luke gospel's deficiencies concerning this census, see Excursus I, 'The Census of Quirinius,' in Schurer's *History of the Jewish People* (1973 ed.), pp. 400–27."

32. *The Jewish Encyclopedia* states that "the connection of Herod with the alleged massacre of the innocents as related in the New Testament is now generally admitted by independent Christian thinkers to be legendary" (s.v. "Herod I"). The historian Charles Guignebert writes, "Neither the visit of the Magi, nor the appearance of the miraculous star, nor the massacre of the innocents has any other basis than the imagination of the hagiographer who put the whole story together." Guignebert, *Jesus* (London, 1935), p. 93; quoted in Barclay, *Introduction to the First Three Gospels*, p. 233.

33. Feminists make much of the Gnostics' attribution of female, as well as male, characteristics of the deity, and for the allegedly pro-female orientation of the Gnostic church; see, for example, Elaine Pagels, *The Gnostic Gospels* (New York: Vantage Books, 1981). This gives them a useful mallet for beating male church leaders about the head. Feminists prefer simply to ignore Gnostic passages that show quite the opposite: for example, "secret saying" 114 reads: "Simon Peter said to them, 'Let Mary leave us, for women are not worthy of life.' Jesus said, 'I myself shall lead her in order to make her male, so that she too may become a living spirit resembling you males. For every woman who will make herself male will enter the Kingdom of

Heaven.' " Pagels (*The Gnostics Gospels*, pp. 80–81) strains to reconcile this passage with the Gnostics' supposed equality of the sexes, suggesting it should be understood "symbolically" as a contrast of the human with the divine.

34. *The Jewish Encyclopedia*, s.v. "Adultery." See also the article "Bastard."

35. *Parade* magazine (December 24, 1989) states, "Castro was born the illegitimate son of his father's cook. Noriega was born the illegitimate son of his father's maid."

36. Jesus' sexual interest in Mary Magdalene is indicated in the long-lost Gnostic book, The Gospel of Philip, 63:32–64:5, in the *Nag Hammadi Library*; see also Pagels, *The Gnostic Gospels*, chapter 3.

37. Hoffmann, *Jesus Outside the Gospels*, pp. 41–42: "The floating tradition concerning the woman taken in adultery (John 7:53–8:11), if part of the Mary-tradition, may point to an early stratum when Mary the mother of Jesus and Mary of Magdala were one and the same. In any case, the gospel tradition concerning the latter Mary may have emerged as a corrective to the story that Jesus' mother was an adulteress." About the two Maries, Hoffmann notes, "even the Gospels offer confused reports."

38. Morton Smith, *The Secret Gospel* (New York: Harper & Row, 1973); *Clement of Alexandria and a Secret Gospel of Mark* (Cambridge, Mass.: Harvard University Press, 1973). Professor Smith suggests that Jesus' actual intention was to found a "mystery cult," probably with sexual rites, a practice quite widespread in the Greco-Roman world. He suggests that the reason for the rapid growth and spread of Gnostic sects, as well as the reason for their fierce persecution by the "orthodox" groups, was their incorporation of Jesus' "libertine" practices.

39. Clement of Alexandria, *The Instructor* XII.

40. Clement of Alexandria, *Miscellanies* V.10.63,7. His reference is apparently to Matthew 13:11, "It is given unto you to know the mysteries of the kingdom of heaven, but to them it is not given."

41. Hippolytus, *Refutation of Heresies* 7:30; quoted by Barclay, *Introduction to the First Three Gospels*, p. 117.

42. Raymond E. Brown, *The Anchor Bible—The Gospel According to John* (New York: Doubleday & Company, 1966), p. 423.

43. Smith, *Clement of Alexandria and a Secret Gospel of Mark*, p. 119.

44. Origen, *Contra Celsum* 1:69.

45. *The Jewish Encyclopedia* says that King Herod I became "abhorrent to the Jews, who could not forgive him for insulting their religious feelings by forcing upon them heathen games and combats with wild animals" (s.v. "Herod I"). The *Encyclopaedia Judaica Jerusalem* states: "Many Jews who wanted to participate nude in the Greek games in the gymnasia underwent painful operations to obliterate the signs of circumcision (*epispasm*). Nevertheless, they aroused the derision and scorn of those whom they imitated" (s.v. "Circumcision").

46. See the Community Rule VII, in G. Vermes, ed., *The Dead Sea Scrolls in English* (Baltimore: Penguin Books, 1966).

47. "All men are either Jews or Hellenes—men with ascetic, picture-hating drives that crave spiritualization, or men with a life-loving . . . and realistic character." *Heinrich Heine über Ludwig Borne*, book 1, in Walter Kaufmann, *Nietzsche* (Princeton, N.J.: Princeton University Press, 1974), p. 377.

48. *The Interpreter's Bible*, vol. 8, p. 10.

49. Gibbon, *Decline and Fall of the Roman Empire*, chapter XXI (Modern Library ed.), vol. 1, p. 690.

50. *Irenaeus Against Heresies* III: 17. This was written around the year 185.

5

The Making of the Messiah, Part Three: The Post-Resurrection Appearances

"If Christ be not risen, then is our preaching vain, and your faith is also vain."
1 Corinthians 15:14

The third major fabrication of the early Christian evangelists involves the alleged "post-Resurrection appearances" of Jesus. In his *Contra Celsum*, written around the year 235, Origen wrote that "people who malign Jesus say his disciples did not see him after he rose from the dead."[1] Many of the surviving portions of "apocryphal" gospels claiming apostolic origin are said to give "legendary expansions at 2 points where the canonical narratives apparently did not satisfy popular demand—Jesus' birth and childhood and his appearances following his Resurrection."[2] Thus, we now see another major problem faced by the early evangelists: the extreme "softness" of their evidence that Jesus had actually risen. Once again they splendidly rose to the occasion, inventing new passages for their various "sacred" scriptures to claim that their risen Messiah had actually been *seen* after his death.

The century before Origen, Celsus charged that "while in the body," Jesus "preached without restraint to all, but when he would establish a strong faith after rising from the dead, he appeared secretly to just one woman and to those of his own confraternity." Significantly, while disputing the details of Celsus' statement, *Origen does not challenge Celsus' assertion that Jesus was not widely seen after the supposed Resurrection,* and strains to cast Jesus' strange post-Resurrection shyness in a favorable light. Origen concedes that "before his passion Jesus appeared quite generally to the crowds," but "after his passion he no longer appeared in the same way, but with deliberate care measured out to each individual that which was right."[3] Jesus realized, according to Origen, that some people "had not the capacity to see him," and he suggests that Jesus may have been concerned that those who disbelieved in his Resurrection might be "smitten with blindness," should he appear in their midst. Origen, the supreme Apologist (the Apologetic movement being that attempt to reconcile the inane simplicity of the early Christian faith with sophisticated Greek and Roman philosophy), suggests that after Jesus' supposed Resurrection, he "no longer had anything about him that could be seen by the multitude."

This, if accepted, would explain why Jesus was not seen by crowds after his death as he regularly had been before. Apparently even Jesus' disciples could tolerate only so much of him: "for not even with the apostles was he always present or always apparent, but because they were unable to receive his divinity without some periods of relief."[4] Thus, by Origen's own admission, the Jesus allegedly seen *after* the Resurrection was not as fully real as the Jesus routinely seen by crowds before. He was instead a sort of phantom said to appear here and there to select persons, and not the living man who had been witnessed by multitudes as he walked from place to place. In the second century, Marcion offered a different solution to the lack of evidence for a Resurrection. He taught that Jesus' body, which had simply appeared on the earth fully grown, disappeared equally abruptly at the time of his death, so that "nothing remained on the tree."[5]

Reading these compromising admissions from one of the most influential Fathers of the early Christian church, any experienced skeptic immediately "smells a rat close by." This same shyness, this exclusiveness, is displayed by all allegedly paranormal phenomena when one attempts to place them under close scrutiny. Thus, the "post-Resurrection Jesus" has much in common with ESP, UFOs, Bigfoot, and the Loch Ness Monster. These are all highly dubious phenomena that tend to dissipate when examined critically. I have already written about UFOs as a *jealous phenomenon,* one that is "suspiciously careful or watchful" in allowing itself to be observed. It will either reveal itself, or hide, depending on who is watching.[6] Clearly, the early Christians recognized that the evidence offered for Jesus' alleged Resurrection was an issue on which they were extremely vulnerable. This caused the Holy Ghost to work overtime, providing inspiration for evangelists generating reams of new problem-solving passages. The only reasonable conclusion we can draw from the "softness" of this evidence is that *there was no Resurrection,* and that the scattered and inconsistent stories of post-Resurrection sightings were made up much later to "prove" that it had occurred.

THE PAULINE ACCOUNT

To Paul—the earliest Christian writer—Jesus' Resurrection was more of a spiritual event than a physical one. When Paul is said to have encountered the risen Jesus along the road to Damascus (Acts 26:13), it was a vision seen by a lone man in the heat of noon in the desert. As such, it has no more probative value than contemporary accounts of encounters with a living Elvis Presley, or the many tales of abductions by aliens in flying saucers. Nietzsche writes scornfully: "To regard as honest a Paul whose home was the principal center of Stoic enlightenment when he makes of a hallucination the *proof* that the redeemer is *still* living, would be a real *niaiserie* on the part of a psychologist: Paul willed the end, *consequently* he willed the means. What he himself did not believe was believed by the idiots among whom he cast *his* teaching—*his* requirement was *power.*"[7]

Whether we regard Paul as sincere or as cynically manipulative, Nietzsche's point is well taken: Paul's reported encounter with the risen Jesus was at best simply a vision, and at worst a lie. When Paul in 1 Corinthians 15:5–8 depicts the post-Resurrection sightings of Jesus by Peter, James, the other apostles, and "five hundred brethren" as indistinguishable from his own, it suggests that all those experiences were subjective and/or hallucinatory. First Corinthians 15:35–50 clearly depicts the Resurrection as a spiritual, not a physical, event: "flesh and blood cannot inherit the kingdom of God . . . the trumpet shall sound, and the dead shall be raised incorruptible, and we shall be changed." Jesus' alleged Resurrection is depicted as not being in any way different than that awaiting all others; indeed, it is called the "first fruits" of mass resurrections to follow. Paul thus seems to be saying that Jesus' physical body remains in the grave, but Jesus' spirit has been appearing to the faithful. We must remember, too, that the Pauline account predates the gospels. Interestingly, Paul always wrote of Jesus' Resurrection using the passive voice. "The uniform terminology of Paul is not that Christ rose from the dead, but that he had been raised by God. The King James version obscures this by translating the passive voice as if the verb were deponent and translating as Christ rose and is risen."[8]

THE GOSPEL ACCOUNTS

We recall that if the Toldoth's account of the Resurrection story is in any way credible, then the "evidence" for Jesus' Resurrection originally consisted of the absence of a body, and nothing more. The unsophisticated early disciples convinced themselves that if Jesus' body was not to be found where it had been left before the Sabbath, well, then he must have ascended into Heaven, exactly as he said he would! While there were, no doubt, many who were perfectly willing to believe that story on such preposterous evidence, with simple childlike hearts, nevertheless, to those of a more philosophical bent prosaic explanations readily suggested themselves. Hence, to silence the impious voices pointing out the extreme "softness" of this evidence, tales of post-Resurrection sightings were invented, and included in—or appended to—each of the four Gospels.

However, because these yarns were relatively late fabrications, the accounts are inconsistent across the four Gospels. Even though Matthew, Mark, and Luke are "Synoptic" Gospels, the story of how the disciples discovered the Resurrection, and of the post-Resurrection appearances of Jesus, do not agree among them. The Synoptics are not "synoptic" in this matter! This clearly indicates that the post-Resurrection stories were invented quite independently, because if this material had been in Mark at the time the other gospels were derived from it, the three would agree on this matter as they do on so many others. For example, the cruci-fiction yarn was already well-established by the time the first gospel was written, resulting in largely consistent accounts across all four. In all probability, the post-Resurrection accounts were composed for the four gospels by different individuals, in different places and times, who may not have had the literary invention of his other brethren before him when he took pen in hand to add details that the Apostle had forgotten to record, details to meet the objections that were everywhere being raised by unbelievers such as Celsus.

In Mark 16:1-8, Mary Magdalene, Mary "the mother of James" (the mother of Jesus' brother had not yet become "a virgin" in this, the earliest gospel), and Salome (/not the daughter of Herodias— her identity is something of a puzzle), walk toward the tomb. They discuss how they might roll away the great stone covering the entrance, and are surprised to find the stone already moved. *Harper's Bible Commentary* suggests that "the stress on the large stone may be an answer to the charge that the disciples stole Jesus' body away."[9] They look inside, and encounter a man clothed in a white garment, who tells them that Jesus is risen. They depart, unwilling to say anything to anyone about this, for "they were afraid."

The original Gospel of Mark ends at this point; *manuscripts of Mark that still survive plainly end here.* All New Testament scholars concede this point. In fact, "it is doubtful if Luke's and Matthew's copies of Mark went beyond 16:8."[10] No doubt it was to meet the objection that nobody actually *saw* a resurrected Jesus that these additional verses were fabricated much later and attributed to Mark, "proving" the reality of the risen Christ. Actually, several different endings were composed to follow Mark 16:8, the most popular ones known as the Shorter and Longer Endings; the Longer Ending is found in most of our Bibles today. In the Longer Ending of Mark, the risen Jesus appears first to Mary Magdalene. Next he appears to two disciples, then to the eleven disciples as they are eating. Jesus speaks words of encouragement to them, and "he [is] received up into heaven," right then and there, on the evening of the day of the Resurrection.

Mark 16:7, in which the risen Jesus' subsequent appearance to Peter in Galilee is predicted, is adjudged to be doubtful as well. Furthermore, Mark 14:28, which predicts future appearances of a risen Jesus in Galilee, is missing from one very ancient Marcan fragment, suggesting that it, too, was not in the original manuscript.[11] The existence of these two questionable passages predicting a risen Jesus in Galilee suggests an intermediate stage in the development of the Marcan Resurrection narratives. Initially, there were no such narratives at all. The two predictive verses were added later, suggesting that the risen Jesus was to be seen in Galilee, perhaps better to meet the objection that nobody saw him anywhere near Jerusalem where he died. Finally, full-blown post-Resurrection sightings are described, apparently in Jerusalem, in the Longer Ending of Mark.

In Matthew, Mary Magdalene and "the other Mary"—presumably the one who has just become a virgin—approach the tomb. (In another of the rare Matthean deletions from Mark, "Salome" was pointedly written out of the story. Perhaps this was because of her connection with the youth who may have been Jesus' lover.) There is "a great earthquake," and they see "the angel of the Lord" come down from heaven to roll back the stone at the front of the tomb. Soon, Jesus appears to both Maries.

Matthew 28:11-15 clearly attempts to refute a Jewish interpretation of the supposed Resurrection. It claims that some soldiers who were on watch at the tomb witnessed Jesus being adored by the two Maries, and reported this to the chief priests and the elders of Israel. They in turn are said to have given "large money" to the soldiers to say that Jesus' disciples had moved his body at night, and to give such testimony to the governor. "So they took the money, and did as they were taught: and this saying is commonly reported among the Jews until this day." This argument would, of course, be pointless if a living Jesus had actually been widely *seen* after his execution; that there was much dispute about what became of Jesus' body strongly suggests that for a long period of time, the absence of a body was the *only* evidence claimed for a Resurrection. Matthew follows through on Mark's prophecy that the risen Jesus would be seen in Galilee, further evidence that the author of Matthew had not seen the Longer Ending of Mark, which places Jesus around Jerusalem. Jesus' disciples go to Galilee, following Jesus' instructions to go to a certain mountain. Jesus appeals to his eleven disciples there, although inexplicably "some [of them] doubted" (Matthew 28:17). When—or if—Jesus ascended into Heaven is not stated.

In Luke 24:1-10, Mary Magdalene, Mary "the mother of James," Joanna, and certain unspecified "other women" go to the tomb. (This solves the conflict between the accounts of Mark and Matthew concerning Salome.) They find the stone already rolled away, and enter the empty tomb. There they encounter not one, but two men in "shining garments," who proclaim to them that Jesus is risen. They go and tell this to the male disciples, who do not believe them. For this point on (24:13), Luke uses no material whatsoever from Matthew or from Mark; he must have reached down deeply into his inexhaustibly rich vein of Q to obtain the forty-one verses that follow.

Luke's post-Resurrection sightings begin not in Galilee, but in the village of Emmaus, about seven miles from Jerusalem. This location might have been chosen to meet the objection that nobody saw Jesus in Galilee, either. In Luke 24:6, an angel pointedly implies that Jesus would not be found in Galilee. Later that day two disciples encounter Jesus in Emmaus, but curiously fail to recognize him. He sits down to dinner with them there, blesses the bread, and "vanishe[s] out of their sight" (Luke 24:31). That evening, Jesus appears to all eleven disciples in Jerusalem as they are eating. Terrified, they think they are seeing a spirit. Jesus speaks to them, citing the prophecy of his Resurrection. To prove he is not a spirit, he eats a fish. Jesus leads the apostles out to Bethany, blesses them, and, as they watch, he rises up to heaven, on the evening of day on which he resurrected. Note how the author of Luke tightly constrains the whereabouts of the risen Jesus so as to restrict his appearances to the disciples, and no one else. Jesus directs them to stay within the city until they are "clothed with power from on high" (Luke 24:49, Revised Standard Version). Clearly, the author of Luke knew that he had to have all of the disciples stay together in Jerusalem—and not go to Galilee— because the Holy Ghost would be coming down, and they all needed to be there to receive It (Acts 2:1–4).[12] Note how the Longer Ending of Mark reflects the Lucan post-Resurrection sightings (cf. Luke 24:13–36 and Mark 16:12–18). This suggests that the author of Luke very likely also wrote the Longer Ending of Mark.

In chapter 20 of John, Mary Magdalene goes to the tomb alone, before sunrise, and finds the stone rolled away. She discovers that the body is missing, and as she runs back she encounters Peter. He returns to the tomb with her. Peter then leaves, and as Mary Magdalene stands outside the tomb, weeping, she sees two angels in white sitting in the tomb where the body had been. They ask her why she is weeping. She answers them, then turns around, and encounters Jesus himself standing there, but she fails to recognize him. She supposes he must be the gardener, and says to him that if he has moved the body, she wishes to know where it is. (Here we see that the author of John is sensitive to the Resurrection story as told in the Toldoth, and seeks to accommodate it.) Jesus speaks to her, and she then recognizes him. Mary Magdalene goes and tells the disciples what has happened. That evening, the disciples are hiding behind locked doors presumably in or near Jerusalem, for fear of what might happen to them, when Jesus suddenly appears among them.

Chapter 21 of John, which contains numerous additional accounts of the risen Jesus being widely seen, is known to New Testament scholars as "the Epilogue" of John. This chapter "is regarded by many scholars as an appendix added by a different hand,"[13] or else by the same hand at a later time. That hand—whoever it was—was obviously extremely eager to "prove" that Jesus was seen many times after his claimed Resurrection. He was likewise eager to identify "the

Beloved Disciple" with John himself (John 21:24), to set to rest the suggestion that he might be Jesus' young lover. In the Epilogue of John, these new post-Resurrection sightings take place at "the sea of Tiberias," i.e., Galilee, the apparent intention being to come into conformity with Matthew's account.

A fundamental difference in the post-Resurrection account exists between the Synoptics and John. The Synoptic post-Resurrection Jesus behaves much like a living person, and is said to have physically ascended into heaven. The risen Jesus in John is much more like that described by Paul, a phantom appearing from time to time to select persons, whose body never actually ascends to heaven, and whose sporadic post-Resurrection appearances just might continue indefinitely.

In John, Jesus' post-Resurrection body would appear and disappear at will. Thomas, who was not with the disciples when Jesus materialized, later refused to believe their account. Eight days afterward, when Thomas was with the disciples, Jesus once again materialized inside a locked room, and "doubting Thomas" was duly convinced. There we see additional disagreement between the Synoptics and the Gospel of John. While in the Synoptics, Jesus' post-Resurrection sojourn on earth appears to have been a single day, John clearly requires a duration of at least eight days. The problem was not "fixed" until the Ascension story was written for Acts, generally attributed to the author of Luke, which gave Jesus forty days on earth after his claimed Resurrection.

THE ASCENSION STORY IN ACTS

If, as is generally believed, Luke and Acts were indeed written by the same author, it is bizarre that he should contradict himself on a matter as important as the Ascension. It may be that the author of Luke wrote the Resurrection story in his gospel before he read what was in John, and later wrote the story of the Ascension now in Acts, seeking to reconcile the two accounts. Significantly, a number of ancient manuscipts of Luke omit the passage "and was carried up into heaven,"[14] in an obvious attempt to come into conformity with Acts 1:9. After the author of Luke wrote that account in Acts, it might be that he or a later redactor tried to *erase* Jesus' ascension in Luke 24:51 from as many copies of the earlier work as he could lay his hands on.

Evangelists and theologians faced a problem in that if the post-Resurrection sightings of Jesus were thought to be in no way different from the visions accompanying all religious experience, the belief that something truly miraculous had happened after Jesus' death would be undermined. John would have no problem with a Jesus whose appearances might go on for centuries, while the Synoptics imply that Jesus' risen body remained only very briefly on earth, all the better to explain why so few people saw it. But John had already proclaimed that the risen Jesus' appearances extended over at least eight days. The first chapter of Acts fixes that problem with a final act of Synoptic fiat: the risen Jesus is now given precisely forty days to work miracles on earth, and is then carried up to heaven, to the accompaniment of an angelic commentary.

Many, perhaps most, New Testament scholars hold that the "Acts of the Apostles" is the sequel to the Gospel of Luke, and that both are by the same author. This statement may well contain some truth, but there are serious problems with it as well. The influential biblical scholar Adolf Harnack dated Acts to about 60–64,[15] earlier than any of the gospels. Of course, other scholars insist it was written much later. But Acts ends with the Apostle Paul still living—he died around the year 64—and under house arrest by the Romans. Paul is still receiving visitors, his eventual fate apparently not known to the author. It is believed by many scholars that Paul, after being released by the Romans, went back to Ephesia and visited Spain before he was finally martyred. Peter, who died around the same time as Paul, is likewise represented as still living. Luke, the latest of the three Synoptic Gospels, appears to have been written twenty or thirty years after Paul's death. Thus, if we assume Luke predates Acts, any reasonable date for the Gospel of Luke makes the date of composition for Acts too late to be plausible, and any date for Acts early enough to account for its content contradicts everything we know about the order and date of the Synoptics.

Many scholars, however, accept a "two authors" interpretation of Acts. There are more substantial variations in still-existing manuscripts of Acts than in any other New Testament book, suggesting multiple authors and/or redactors. In any case, it cannot in any way be established that Luke, said to be the companion of Paul, wrote the Gospel of Luke. The problem can be solved if we assume that an early manuscript of Acts, written during Paul's lifetime, was substantially expanded and revised much later by the same author who produced Luke. If we call this hypothetical early manuscript

A, then we see that the author of Luke twice created a new and improved book from a less sophisticated older version: from Mark he produced Luke, and from A he produced Acts. Acts did not appear publicly in the churches until the middle of the second century.

Acts is interesting for a number of reasons. This is the only place in the New Testament outside the gospels (other than the "nonphysical" sightings in 1 Corinthians 15) where a post-Resurrection appearance of Jesus is described. The first chapter of Acts is also remarkable in that it is the only place outside the Synoptic Gospels where we find mention of Mary, the mother of Jesus; otherwise, the question of Jesus' parents is scrupulously avoided. Paul says that Jesus was born "of a woman" (Galatians 4:4), but prefers not to name her, probably because he does not want to deal with the problem of "Miriam M'gadella."

THE TOLDOTH ACCOUNT

Let us return to the account of what happened after Jesus' death as recounted in the *Toldoth Jeshu,* which I described in chapter 1. First, we note that it has Jesus not being "entombed" at all, but simply buried in an earthen grave. Presumably the first Christian "improvement" to the Resurrection story was to invent a tomb, sealed by a massive stone, to make it seem less plausible that Jesus' body could have simply been moved. This may explain why Paul seems to know nothing of the "empty tomb" story, while Mark, writing fifteen years later, makes so much of it; it had not yet been made up at the time of the genuine Pauline epistles. When stories of the "empty tomb," sealed by a massive stone, were found insufficiently convincing, actual post-Resurrection encounters were then invented.

If we accept the Toldoth's account that the gardener moved Jesus' body between the time it was buried and the time when the disciples arrived, we perceive at once that this gardener has created a very significant problem for himself. Jesus was slain and hanged in a tree on a Friday, which also happened to be the eve of Passover.* Jesus' body was hastily taken down and buried before sunset, so that "thy land be not defiled," especially not on the eve of a doubly holy day (Passover and Sabbath). During the Sabbath—from sundown on Fri-

---

*While the Christian celebration of Easter always occurs on a Sunday, the Jewish celebration of Passover can occur on any day of the week.

day to sundown the following day—virtually all normal activities are suspended, except for those associated with religious observances. Thus, if the gardener drained an irrigation channel, dug a hole under it and moved Jesus' body into this hole, then filled in the hole and refilled the channel with water—a lengthy process to be sure—*he did all this on the Sabbath,* and indeed on the day of Passover, one of the most sacred days of the Jewish calendar. He had committed a sin "deserving of death" according to the Mosaic law! The Toldoth does not raise this issue. Presumably the gardener hoped that his neighbors would all be in the Temple and would not notice his impiety.

Now imagine the dilemma this presumed vegetable farmer would have faced the following day. The Sabbath is over, and it is the disciples' first opportunity to visit Jesus' grave.[16] They are shocked to discover an empty hole in the ground where the body had been buried. (The Toldoth does not say precisely what the disciples discovered, but obviously a body will not be noted as missing unless the grave is open.) Within hours, the entire town, and probably many other towns in the immediate vicinity, were aflame with excited talk of Jesus' presumed Resurrection. Surely, the gardener never imagined that moving a dead body would stir up such a fuss.

But what should he do now? If he says nothing, the preposterous nonsense being preached by "the insurgents of Israel" will continue to spread, to the great distress of all law-abiding Jews. But if he explains what has happened, *by his own words he convicts himself of a capital offense!* What would *you* do in a dilemma like that? If the Toldoth can be believed—and in this matter it makes more sense than any other account—the gardener apparently hesitated for days or perhaps even weeks, to mull things over, although that book does not speculate on his motives. Eventually, he decided to confess what had happened, thereby confronting whatever shame or punishment might be his due: perhaps even death!

Whether such a garden and a gardener actually existed, we cannot say for sure. However, the second-century "apocryphal" Gospel of Peter says that Jesus was interred in a tomb *in a garden* belonging to Joseph of Arimathea. Moreover, Hugh Schonfield cites other ancient sources that seem to lend credibility to the role of a supposed "gardener." He writes: "In the British Museum (Orient MSS. 6804) is a Coptic script entitled *The Book of the Resurrection,* attributed to the Apostle Bartholomew. In this document the Jews, after the crucifixion, are looking for a safe place to deposit the body of Jesus so that the disciples will not steal it secretly."[17] A gardener named

Philogenes agrees to place the body in a tomb and watch over it, while actually intending to take it elsewhere and anoint it for burial. However, when Philogenes goes to the tomb at midnight, he discovers it filled with angels, the Resurrection events being already underway.

Schonfield also adduces a ninth-century work by Agobard, Archbishop of Lyons, titled *De Judaici Superstitionibus* (*On Jewish Superstitions*). In this work, Agobard "cites the teachings of the Jewish elders who set down in writing that after Jesus was hanged, 'he was buried by a canal, and handed over to a certain Jew to guard. By night, however, he was carried away by the sudden overflowing of the canal, and though he was sought for twelve months by the order of Pilate, he could never be found.' . . . By Agobard's 'canal' we are to understand an irrigation channel serving the plantation or vegetable plot, a very appropriate feature."[18]

Note how in Agobard's account, the loss of Jesus' body was simply an unfortunate accident. It is thus possible that a heavy rain, or a failure in a lock, or a careless error in opening flood gates, may have washed Jesus' body into a river and out to sea. Schonfield wisely cautions against relying too much on accounts of this kind. However, from what we have seen, it is eminently reasonable to conclude that the gospel accounts of the Resurrection are based on Christian belief, not on historical fact. The original "evidence" for a Resurrection was simply the inability to locate Jesus' body. The actions of some gardener growing vegetables, whether deliberate or not, may have caused the body to be moved.

According to the Toldoth, the body of Jesus was ultimately located, and it was dragged through the streets of Jerusalem on a rope behind a horse. This claim, while at first sight utterly bizarre, repugnant, and unthinkable to those indoctrinated in Christian orthodoxy, is supported by both Jewish and Moslem texts. *The Jewish Encyclopedia* says "this insult offered to [Jesus'] body in the streets of Jerusalem is also alluded to in the Koran."[19] It is possible, however, that these two are not independent sources; there are reasons for believing that Muhammad was familiar with the Toldoth. Those who assert the Toldoth to be a "medieval forgery" would no doubt dispute this, but Tertullian, like Celsus and even Muhammad, seems to have known many of the principal arguments of the Toldoth, if not the book itself; Tertullian shows himself sensitive to the Jews' assertion that a gardener moved Jesus' body.[20]

During the time between the disappearance of Jesus' body and its reported rediscovery, news of Jesus' presumed Resurrection would have spread far and wide. There were no newspapers or photographs in the ancient world, so it was difficult for anyone to establish what had actually happened: everything depended on whose account you believed. If Jesus' body actually was dragged behind a horse through the streets of Jerusalem, those who saw it knew that the Resurrection story was not true, but those who heard about it second-hand could not be so sure. "One man says that Jesus arose from the dead, but another says that his body was found and dragged through the streets. I myself have seen neither—which story should I believe?" No doubt multitudes of people faced that same dilemma, centuries before William of Occam formulated his famous "razor" for evaluating competing explanations.[21] Belief in Jesus' Resurrection presumably began during that relatively brief period between the body being missed and its discovery, spread explosively, and has literally never died out.

DID JESUS WORK MIRACLES?

We cannot conclude our examination of the origins of Christianity without addressing the question of Jesus' alleged "miracles." Obviously, if the descriptions of these accounts are literally correct, Jesus must have possessed some kind of supernatural powers. But before jumping to dramatic conclusions, we must ask ourselves whether it is in fact *necessary* to possess supernatural powers in order to convince multitudes, especially those of little education, that one is a miracle-worker. We must also ask whether the gospel miracle stories have credibility as historically accurate descriptions of real events. The answer to both questions is a resounding no.

A perusal of evangelical television programs having a wide audience today will make it clear that every kind of "miracle" attributed to Jesus is *reported* to be duplicated by faith healers today—even resurrection of the dead!—and that millions of people believe them. Given the lower standards of education and critical thinking prevailing two millennia ago, it must then have been even easier to fool the unsophisticated than it is today. And today's miracle mongers are still not finding it difficult. We must remember that it was the ignorant, not the learned, who were Jesus' most ardent disciples, exactly the stratum of society most thoroughly taken in by present-day bamboozlers. It is abundantly clear from what we know of social history that practically any unscrupulous person who is a good speaker can convince multitudes that he can work miracles. Furthermore, because of the natural human tendency to exaggerate the remarkable, the accounts we hear and read of extraordinary events can be shown to be highly suspect even when dealing with that which is claimed in recent years; imagine how much more unreliable are accounts many centuries older than that.

Worse yet, many of the gospel miracle stories appear simply to be retellings of Old Testament miracles, utilizing similar or even virtually identical language. This demonstrates beyond any doubt that these accounts are stylized fictional constructs, and not descriptions of real events. Randel Helms shows conclusively in *Gospel Fictions* that many of the principal miracle stories about Jesus are practically copies of Old Testament miracle accounts from the Septuagint, the Greek-language translation of Hebrew Scripture that was widely read by the earliest Christians.

Jesus' miracle at the wedding in Cana (John 2:1–11) is clearly influenced by the account of Elisha providing flour and oil in 1 Kings. Mark's account of Jesus walking on the sea (Mark 6:48) draws from the Septuagint's Greek phrases describing how the Lord "treadeth upon the waves of the sea" (Job 9:8). "All the gospel stories of Jesus' resurrecting a dead loved one are based on the resurrections in the Books of Kings."[22] Helms gives many more such examples. From their reading of the Septuagint, Greek-speaking Christians expected holy persons to perform certain deeds, and so miracle stories were fabricated for the gospels, often using precisely the same phrases, to establish Jesus' celestial credentials. Thus whatever Jesus may have done to convince people that he was a miracle worker (and since even in rabbinical passages "Yeshua ben Panthera" has the reputation of performing prodigious feats, we can safely infer that he claimed such powers), the miracle stories as they appear in the gospels are for the most part literary fictions.

As amazing as it sounds to us today, steeped in centuries of orthodox preaching, it is clear from the gospels that even in the final days of his ministry, after allegedly performing dozens of miracles, Jesus' brothers still did *not* believe in his alleged divine mission or in his miracles! Even after the supposed miracles of the loaves and the fishes, Jesus walking on water, and changing water into wine, John 7:5 informs us: "neither did his brethren believe him." The Synoptics convey this same message. Mark 3:31–35 carries the clear implication that Jesus' disciples, who believed in his miracles, were his true "brethren," not his mother and his brothers, who apparently would not join "the multitude" in following his teachings. This passage is repeated without substantial changes in Matthew 12:46–50 and Luke 8:19–21. That those who knew Jesus better than anyone else— his own immediate family—disbelieved in his alleged miracles at a time when thousands believed in him, should make us immediately suspicious about what Jesus was doing. Their unbelief is especially remarkable since Jesus' mother was said to be at his side when he allegedly changed water into wine (John 2:3–5), assuming there to be any reality to this account. Morton Smith describes with painful accuracy the situation Jesus found himself in:

> Here are details preserved in the gospels to tell us that Jesus was the son of Mary (his father was uncertain), was a carpenter in Nazareth where his family lived, went back for a visit after he had set up as an exorcist, but was regarded with contempt by the townspeople and could do no miracles there. Even his brothers did not believe him, and once, at the beginning of his career, his family and friends tried to put him under restraint as insane. For his part, he rejected them, and had nothing to do with them through all his late career.[23]

It is true that Jesus' brother, known as "James the Just," became a respected leader of the infant Church in the years immediately following the execution of Jesus, a sharp turnaround from the disbelief and disinterest imputed to him earlier. However, it can only be conjectured whether his actions were motivated by genuine belief in Jesus' divinity, or, like Lenin, by the desire to avenge a brother's death at the hands of the state.

Celsus charges that Jesus learned magic in Egypt: "because he was poor he hired himself out as a workman in Egypt, and there tried his hand at certain magical powers on which the Egyptians pride themselves; he returned full of conceit because of these powers, and on account of them he gave himself the title of God."[24] There are a number of passages in the Talmud saying essentially the same thing.[25] Matthew's Infancy Narrative seeks to accommodate what seems to have been the widely known fact of Jesus going off to Egypt during his youth.

These ancient critics were given to understand that while in Egypt Jesus learned to cast spells, but what I am suggesting is that while in Egypt he learned to produce *illusions*. Magic as it is understood today—creating the appearance of an impossible event through sleight of hand, misdirection, or trickery—had its origins in Egypt thousands of years ago. Most of the tricks magicians use today are based on principles perfected in ancient Egypt and India. With sophisticated techniques of misdirection and sleight-of-hand, the magician can furtively substitute one object for another, making it appear that a magical transformation has taken place. He can likewise pull a concealed object from an unexpected hiding place, or hide an object previously seen, thereby seeming to have the power of making objects appear and disappear at will.

We do not know the precise circumstances under which Jesus' alleged miracles occurred, or what opportunities for creating illusions did, or did not, exist; the gospels simply assert that they happened. Jesus is said to have fed five thousand men on five barley loaves and two fishes (John 6:9–13). Even today, however, Indian "God-Men" acquire thousands of devoted followers by appearing to produce food from nowhere. In actuality, the "Faker" has stored a copious quantity of food under a table, hidden from sight. The "God-Man" appears to reach into the air for the food, but it is actually handed to him by an assistant who is likewise concealed. Jesus allegedly changed water into wine (John 2:7–10). But magicians routinely "change" one liquid into another in performances today. Did Jesus perform his "miracles" in this manner? Or are the gospel accounts wholly fictional, a retelling of Old Testament wonders? We cannot say for sure.

CONCLUSION: THE MAKING OF THE MESSIAH

We can at last begin to see the outline of a more believable, more *parsimonious* story of the life of Jesus, one that is for the most part consistent with the few extant historical sources that are credible, especially those sources *outside* the Gospels. It is a story which does no violence to common sense:

A young girl in Nazareth of Galilee, perhaps as young as four-teen, is betrothed to a carpenter much older than herself. He spends much time away from home. Before they are married, she becomes pregnant by a Roman soldier named Panthera, who is a Gentile. This creates a scandal; the carpenter denounces her, and they soon part company forever. Because of the shame associated with her illegitimate pregnancy, the girl's family runs her out and no one is willing to shelter her. She wanders from place to place. When the time comes for her to deliver her child, she takes refuge in a stable.

Her son, who is known as Yeshua ben Panthera, is a social outcast because his mother is an adulteress. He thus nurses a sullen resentment against the laws and customs of the Jewish nation, and begins to display an open contempt for its religious leaders and traditions. This causes him to be perceived as "wicked" by all who revere those laws. However, he becomes a hero to "the insurgents of Israel," to anyone who carries around a grudge against the status quo, for whatever reason.

Because Yeshua—in Latin, Jesus—is treated badly in Jewish society, he goes off to live for many years in the Greek-speaking world which at that time dominated the eastern Mediterranean. He adopts Greek practices of which pious Jews did not approve, such as wrestling and taking a male lover. Apparently Jesus spent some time in Egypt, which then had many Greek-speaking cities. While there, he learned magic illusions, with which he was easily able to deceive simple folk. His self-confidence bolstered by his new skills, he returned to Galilee and Judea seeking to triumph over those who had earlier despised him.

Jesus performed clever illusions such as the animation of clay birds, and the production of food from "nowhere," much as magicians perform them today. Using the techniques of suggestion that are still employed by contemporary faith healers, Jesus acquired the reputation of a great magician and healer. The huge following of this "insurgent," who claimed his laws took precedence over all established religious authority, generated so much civil unrest that Jesus was arrested. On the eve of Passover, he was tried by the Sanhedrin for leading the people "astray," found guilty, and executed by stoning, all in accordance with Jewish law. His body was hung on a tree until sunset, when it was taken down and buried. The following day—the Passover *and* the Sabbath—no secular activity was permitted, but a gardener might have been busy at work nonetheless. Somehow, Jesus' body was moved.

When the sun rose on the first day of the week, it being once again lawful to resume normal activity, Jesus' disciples were astonished to find that his body had disappeared. They assumed that he must have ascended into heaven, in accordance with prophecy. Within days or even hours, all of Israel was ablaze with reports of the supposed Resurrection. Some time later— perhaps much later—the body may have been discovered and dragged through the streets of Jerusalem behind a horse, where many people saw it, but far fewer than the number who had heard of the supposed "Resurrection." Belief in the Resurrection of Jesus never disappeared, and a new religion was born, one nurtured by the resentments of those who chafed beneath the burden of conformity to Mosaic law.

This new belief spread rapidly among "the insurgents of Israel," but it offered little to interest the Gentiles, who were not subject to Jewish religious law, and hence derived no gratification from seeing it successfully challenged. However, by altering the circumstances of Jesus' death to claim victory over the Romans' hated cross, Christianity was soon augmented by "the insurgents" among the Gentiles, enthralling everyone who, for whatever reason, nursed a grudge against the power, refinement, and wealth that was Rome.

As the new religion grew in size and influence, claiming Jesus as the Messiah expected by the Jews, many objections were raised to its teachings by Jews and other critics. Because they uniformly objected to a bastard being the Messiah, stories of a supernatural conception and a Davidic genealogy were subsequently fabricated on Jesus' behalf. When major problems were found with that genealogy, a second one was written to emend the most serious problems in the first. Jesus' birthplace was likewise "moved" from Nazareth to Bethlehem to conform to prophecy, by the invention of two contrived (and mutually inconsistent) nativity stories.

The first "proof" of the Resurrection was simply the absence of Jesus' body. Because that account was challenged on the grounds that Jesus' body had probably been moved, a heavy tomb, covered by a massive stone, was invented. When it was further objected that Jesus' Resurrection was merely *inferred* from the missing body, and was not actually witnessed, passages were then written claiming that the risen Jesus had actually been seen. Thus were the Christians' "Holy Scriptures" gradually shaped to meet these and other objections. When the "virgin birth" story became so widely accepted that it was seldom questioned, those Holy Books offering a heroic defense of it—such as the Gospel of Mary, the Protevangelion of James, and the Gospel of Nicodemus—were banished from the Canon because each "doth protest too much." Other books having theological difficulties or judged to have marginal value are banished as well.

Occam's Razor dictates that the above interpretation of the life of Jesus is to be preferred to those which abound in speculative or supernatural elements.

We recall Celsus' charge that the Christians "have corrupted the Gospel from its original integrity, to a threefold, fourfold, and manifold degree, and have remodeled it, so that they might be able to answer objections." O wise and gentle Celsus, you have solved the Synoptic problem!

NOTES

1. Origen, *Contra Celsum* 1:31

2. Lucetta Mowry, "Noncanonical Early Christian Writings," in *The Interpreter's One Volume Commentary*, Charles M. Laymon, ed. (Nashville, Tenn.: Abingdon, 1971), p. 1146.

3. Origen, *Contra Celsum* 1:31.

4. Origen, *Contra Celsum* 2:64–70.

5. *Tertullianus Against Marcion* 4:42:7:9, "Nihil ergo remansit in ligno." *Lignum* might represent a tree, or a wooden structure such as a gibbet.

6. Robert Sheaffer, *The UFO Verdict* (Buffalo, N.Y.: Prometheus Books, 1981, 1986), chapter 16. A *jealous phenomenon* is one that always makes itself scarce before the evidence becomes too convincing.

7. Nietzsche, *Der Antichrist* 42, trans. R. J. Hollingdale (New York: Penguin Books, 1974). For a further discussion of Paul's motives, see Nietzsche's *Die Morgenrote* (*Dawn*, or *Daybreak*) 68, a passage included in Walter Kaufmann's *The Portable Nietzsche* (New York: Penguin Books, 1978).

8. *The Interpreter's Bible* (New York: Abingdon Press, 1951), vol. 10, p. 223.

9. James L. Mays, ed., *Harper's Bible Commentary* (San Francisco: Harper & Row, 1988), commentary on Mark 16.

10. *The Interpreter's Bible*, vol. 7, pp. 914–15.

11. Burton H. Throckmorton, Jr., ed., *Gospel Parallels* (Nashville, Tenn.: Thomas Nelson Publishers, 1979), p. 168. The *Interpreter's Bible*, vol. 7, p. 914, regards both Mark 14:28 and 16:7 as "interpolations," i.e., dubious late additions.

12. To me, this suggests that when the author of Luke wrote his gospel he was already familiar with an older, rudimentary manuscript of Acts, containing the Pentecost story but lacking an Ascension fable, which he later authored. If the Ascension account giving Jesus forty days on earth already existed, the Gospel of Luke would not restrict Jesus to one. Probably after writing Luke 24, but before writing Acts 1, this author read John's account, requiring Jesus to be on earth at least eight days after rising from the dead.

13. *The Interpreters Bible*, vol. 8, p. 446.

14. Throckmorton, *Gospel Parallels*, p. 190.

15. *The Interpreter's Bible*, vol. 9, p. 21.

16. "As soon as that day of stillness was over, at the earliest possible moment, the women are at the tomb, determined to honour the dead as best they may." C. D. F. Moule, *Cambridge Commentary on the New English Bible* (Cambridge, England: Cambridge University Press, 1965), p. 131, on Mark 16:1.

17. Hugh J. Schonfield, *After The Cross* (La Jolla, Calif.: A. S. Barnes & Co., Inc., 1981), pp. 47–49.

18. Ibid., pp. 47, 49.

19. *The Jewish Encyclopedia* (ca. 1905), s.v. "Jesus."

20. Tertullian, *De Spectaculis* 30.

21. Occam's Razor is usually given by its Latin formulation, *Entia non sunt multiplicanda praeter necessitatem* ("No more things should be presumed to exist than are absolutely necessary"). In other words, hypotheses involving extraordinary elements, such as the resurrection of the dead, should not be invoked unless it is completely impossible to account for known facts in any other way. Occam's razor is a cornerstone of the philosophy of science.

22. Randel Helms, *Gospel Fictions* (Buffalo, N.Y.: Prometheus Books, 1988), p. 65.

23. Morton Smith, *Jesus the Magician* (San Francisco: Harper & Row, 1978), p. 27.

24. Origen, *Contra Celsum* 1:28.

25. These are described in *The Jewish Encyclopedia*, s.v. "Jesus: Sojourn in Egypt" and "Jesus as Magician."

6

The First God to Claim a Monopoly

"I the Lord thy God am a jealous God."
Exodus 20:5

MONOTHEISM AND RESENTMENT

Until the invention of monotheism about three thousand years ago, all the religions of the earth were polytheistic. They worshiped a wide assortment of deities, male and female, benevolent and angry, human and animal. Perhaps the most remarkable aspect of polytheism, seen from the perspective of modern-day religious practice, is the virtually complete absence of religious wars, religious disputes, and religious intolerance. Because there was no fixed number of gods and goddesses that might inhabit the upper regions, whatever beliefs one group held were not seen as necessarily conflicting with the different beliefs of another. The sky was, after all, quite vast, and perhaps *both* groups might be worshiping "true" gods, whose functions or domains did not overlap.

Gibbon writes of the "universal toleration of polytheism" in Roman times,[1] which he so artfully contrasts with the fanatical intolerance of the Christians. While the various gods and goddesses of polytheism had their own petty rivalries and squabbles, none of them sought exclusive worship. Indeed, it did not matter even if two or more different and seemingly incompatible systems of polytheism were practiced side by side: proponents of the Greco-Roman, Norse, Egyptian, and Persian religions peacefully coexisted. There were no holy wars, and nobody slaughtered anyone else merely for worshiping the "wrong" gods. If I worship the gods of my country, and you worship the gods of yours, that is no reason for us to argue about anything; in all probability, my gods reign here, and yours there. If we spend a lot of time together, I probably will end up honoring some of your gods, and you some of mine. My country might even adopt one or more of your gods into our religion, and your religion some of ours. Newly imported gods were free to change their roles if that allowed them to fit better into their new environment.

This abundance of deities was felt to be an actual advantage, not a drawback. The Romans ended up with so many gods that they erected the huge and magnificent Pantheon (literally "all gods"), a building still standing today, to show off this proud collection. Statues of each deity, major and minor, were exhibited in the Pantheon, and supplicants were free to make offerings to any one of them in an attempt to obtain favors. These gods were seen as benefactors and protectors of Rome who, while occasionally peevish or petulant, were nonetheless susceptible to bribes of burnt offerings or to flattery. Prosperity, triumph in battle, success in love, domestic tranquility: all were perceived as gifts showered down upon the Roman people by the fundamentally beneficent gods they worshiped.

Some will object to my depiction of Roman religious tolerance by noting that Roman magistrates were not exactly tolerant of Christian religious practices. And this is indeed true. While the frequency and diligence of Roman persecution have been greatly exaggerated by Christian writers, many Christians were indeed martyred for their beliefs, often enduring horrible tortures. Why was Christianity, alone of all religions, singled out for this sporadic but sometimes severe persecution?

The Romans, like all peoples at that time, did not have a separation of church and state. The gods and goddesses honored in the Pantheon were seen as Rome's protectors, and their good graces were courted as necessary for the continued health of the state. Many activities in daily life required one at least to pretend to honor and thank these deities. Foreigners who worshiped other gods could with a clear conscience pour an offering to Jupiter, Zeus, Apollo, or Minerva while visiting Rome; to honor one god did not dishonor any other. It was like paying homage to a king who ruled over some distant land. The educated, who in private viewed all gods as poetic fictions, were happy to make such gestures in public as a demonstration of loyalty to the state.

But only the Christians—and the Jews—obstinately refused to make at least a pretense of honoring these protective deities. Complicating the problem further, the Romans regarded their emperor as at least quasi-divine in life and a full-fledged god after death. Only the Christians and the Jews defiantly refused to salute the emperor in a manner befitting a deity. This was perceived as tantamount to treason against the state. Such behavior by Jews was grudgingly tolerated, primarily because theirs was an ancient religion even two thousand years ago, and the Romans respected those who followed the religion of their forefathers. Another major difference was that while the Jewish religion was not actively seeking proselytes, and hence not expanding, the Christian religion was making great efforts to expand at the fastest possible rate. This made Christian fanaticism seem infinitely more dangerous than its Jewish counterpart. "The painful and even dangerous rite of circumcision was alone capable of repelling a willing proselyte from the door of the synagogue," Gibbon observed wrly,[2] and perhaps that effect was intended; only when such ritual mutilation of the genitals is inflicted on helpless infants can it be performed with impunity, by one generation upon the next.

While Jews and Romans sometimes fought each other fiercely, and Roman Jews were at times subjected to a special tax, the two groups were eventually able to accommodate each other, to live and let live. Jewish merchants played a major role in the Roman economy, and even many non-Jewish merchants began to close up shop on the Sabbath. But Christians were unable to claim the sanction of time and custom for their rapidly expanding sect, and were likewise unable to claim to make major contributions to Rome's prosperity. The Romans saw Christianity as an upstart sect of rebellious proletarians and slaves who were scornful of everything that was sacred and good, whose dangerous doctrines threatened to undermine the very foundations of Roman life. (And eventually it did, with the coming of the likes of Augustine, who argued in his *City of God* that the sack of Rome by barbarians should have been scarcely noted by those whose gaze is fixed on Heaven.) The Romans reacted to Christianity as if it had been custom-crafted with the view of undermining a citizen's participation in the body politic; indeed, a cynic might suggest that it was. If some malicious person, burning with *ressentiment* against Roman wealth and power, sat down to devise a religion that would throw the greatest possible monkey wrench into Roman affairs of state, that religion would need to behave much as Christianity actually did.

As far as we know, the concept of monotheism was first proclaimed about 1375 B.C. by the Egyptian pharaoh Amenhotep IV, a ruler of the Eighteenth Dynasty. The Egyptian sun-god Aton had been rising in prominence in that country's pantheon, and eventually one cult proclaimed Aton the sole, true god. Amenhotep adopted this belief fervently, changed his name to Ikhnaton, and attempted to impose the new religion upon his people. Because an Egyptian pharaoh was an absolute monarch, his monotheism became the official religion of Egypt for a short time, and Ikhnaton set out to purge all temples and inscriptions of other gods. However, the Egyptian people never willingly accepted this imposition of monotheism, and the priesthood put up considerable resistance. Ikhnaton ruled for only seventeen years, and was not well thought of afterward. Following his death, Egypt suffered a period of anarchy in which both its empire and power were diminished. The traditional religious practices were soon restored.

The Israelites were the first people in history fervently to embrace a jealous God who claimed an absolute monopoly on divinity, one who absolutely excluded all other possible supernatural claimants. Probably while in Egypt, the Israelites were greatly influenced by that fanatical zeal of the now disgraced Ikhnaton. Their God asserted unequivocally: "I am the Lord thy God, which have brought thee out of the land of Egypt, out of the house of bondage. Thou shalt have no other gods before me. Thou shalt not make unto thee any graven image, or any likeness of anything that is in heaven above, or that is in the earth beneath, or that is in the water under the earth: Thou shalt not bow down thyself to them, nor serve them; for I the Lord thy God am a jealous God" (Exodus 20:2–5).

Monotheism has almost unquestioningly been regarded as a sign of progress in religion and morality, a sign of a more advanced stage of civilization. I would dispute this. Few have pondered the question of whether the invention of a jealous God should be considered a step forward or a step back in the course of civilization. Certainly from the standpoint of civilized tolerance, we cannot but consider rabid monotheism a step in the wrong direction. Surely it is more likely to lead to unnecessary bloodshed. Indeed, the three major world religions that worship this same jealous God are still furiously fighting each other today in and around that tiny land that all three think

Bedouins, whose life, on the whole, is less "civilized" than that of the earliest Hebrews on record, were suddenly transported to Tel Aviv or Jerusalem."[5]

Thus, the despised "heathen" so reviled in the Jewish Scriptures had a two-thousand year head start in civilization over those who invented an angry God eager to destroy them. In other words, the supposedly "advanced" concept of monotheism had its origins in the vindictiveness of a primitive tribe finding itself surrounded by magnificent, advanced civilizations; of impoverished peoples who labored in the shadows of the pyramids and hanging gardens erected by the most developed societies on earth at the time. Baron cites evidence that even before the Hebrews encountered the Egyptians, their patriarchs probably had already had significant contact with "the mature civilization of Babylonia," and seemed to have roots in Chaldea. Thus they were indeed familiar with—and given the circumstances, almost certainly envious of—advanced civilizations.

Even in Greco-Roman times, most Jews were conspicuously less affluent than their "heathen" neighbors.[6] And what will almost certainly happen when an impoverished, uneducated tribe or nation has large-scale interactions with a civilization centuries or even millennia ahead of themselves in wealth and worldly knowledge? History assures us that the backward tribe will feel an overpowering degree of resentment against the achievements of that civilization, whose wealth, art, and architecture must seem impossibly far beyond all previous imagining. While envy is present to some degree in all societies, it is most prominent in those that are the least developed, that being precisely the factor limiting their success. Only by looking at the unceasing rage of some of today's primitive third-world societies against the wealth and achievements of the democratic, capitalist West can we visualize the degree of malicious rage and envy that the glories of Babylon and Egypt must have stirred up within the primitive Hebrews.

In *Resentment Against Achievement* I wrote, "Speaking very broadly, Christianity was the movement built upon lower-class resentments against the wealth of the Roman Empire, and socialism was built upon resentment against the wealth generated by the industrial revolution."[7] To this we must now add: *Monotheistic Judaism was a movement built upon lower-class resentments against the wealth and power of the advanced civilizations of the ancient Middle East.* In a spiteful act of genius, an envious people created an all-powerful, envious god in their own image.

Thus every major high-water mark of civilization witnesses the birth of an envious value system that works to destroy it. Every time some mighty civilization rises to a pinnacle of power, those who are intensely envious of its success eventually manage to devise, through a process of seemingly endless trial and error, a value system uniquely capable of weakening it. Once perfected, this outlook spreads rapidly, electrifying those who share such resentments. The first freely held monotheistic belief system in the history of the world was thus invented as a kind of slave insurrection. And from that time to our own, the One Jealous God, no matter under what name he is worshiped, has always stood in opposition to highly developed civilizations, castigating them as "worldly." The God preached by every malignant monotheism in the world is born out of resentment against the achievements of some advanced civilization, a role he continues to play to this very day. Such a God will invariably be found in opposition to the progress of science, to unfettered education and commerce, and especially to the sexual fulfillment that a dynamic, cosmopolitan society is wise enough to tolerate.

Consider the fierce anger of Yahweh at the sexual liberty of Sodom and Gomorrah (Genesis 19). This omnipotent Being, who as the supposed creator of us all bears sole responsibility for the strength of our overpowering sexual urges, nonetheless rains down "fire and brimstone" upon those who act upon the very urges he planted. We must remember that in comparison with more civilized, cosmpolitan ancient peoples, the rules of sexual conduct prescribed by the ancient Jews were extremely harsh and unforgiving, especially for women. An adulteress was at risk of being stoned, and the child born to an adulteress would be an outcast all its life, owing to circumstances totally beyond its control.

As the millennia passed and Judaic civilization prospered, these exceedingly harsh rules were gradually softened; all civilized people eventually become more humane. It is virtually always the case that the sexual mores of less advanced peoples are far more rigid and unforgiving than those in whom education and exposure to diverse cultures has inspired tolerance; the more envious a people, the less it is able to endure thoughts of others' bliss. The early Hebrews' horror at the sexual fulfillment of their neighbors is typical of proletarian thought; what is especially unfortunate is that millions have been persuaded that these are not merely the prejudices of primitive nomads, but indubitable pronouncements of the one and Only God. While our knowledge of the biblical Sodom and Gomorrah is obviously extemely limited, we may safely infer that they were rich, cosmopolitan cities that did not subscribe to the exceedingly rigid sexual mores of the ancient Hebrews. Expressing this in modern terms, these cities must have seemed like Paris or San Francisco do today to illiterate country bumpkins, who still employ the Jews' brilliant invention—an envious, begrudging, all-powerful God—as their best hope for putting an end to others' pleasure and wealth.

The ancient religions displaced by jealous monotheisms were, almost invariably, *fertility cults*, that is, religions in which procreation and fertility were major concerns. Ceres (Demeter) was responsible for the success of the grain harvest. The rites of Dionysus (Bacchus) were blatantly sexual, and farther north the orgies associated with the Maypole and the other nature festivals assured the fertility of mankind and crops alike. Without exception, worshipers of the One Jealous God not only discontinued all such fertility-promoting practices, but found them outrageous and abominable, and denounced them in the strongest possible terms. Instead of showering down fertility and fulfillment like the ancient gods of polytheism, the One Jealous God rained down brimstone and the fires of hell.

What *must* one deduce about the motives of any group that is outraged by practices intended to promote fertility? Are we not forced to conclude that the new religions, in opposing fertility, were gratified by barrenness and destitution? And we are expected to hail monotheism as a sign of progress in civilization? I say it represents a colossal step backward! If the ancient religions were cults of fertility, then the jealous monotheisms replacing them must be termed *cults of infertility*, as they become enraged by any practice intended to help people "live long and prosper."

It is at present very fashionable for feminists to speak wistfully of a vanished Golden Age of "goddess worship" in western Asia, an age sadly ended by horrid "patriarchs" whose technological advancements allowed them to oppress and dominate a supposed peace-loving matriarchy, and impose their "patriarchal" religions, such as Christianity, Judaism, and Islam. This vanished Nirvana-on-earth was uniquely blissful, the feminists claim, on the island of Crete, where happy female-led goddess worshipers flourished for centuries in peace, harmony, and equality.

But like all manifestations of *ressentiment*, the tenets of feminism are grounded in spite and delusion, not reality. Feminists are correct to note that the ancient "goddess worshipers" were far more tolerant than Christians, Moslems, or Jews. But this was a trait shared by *all* polytheistic religions, having nothing to do with matriarchs or patriarchs. Worshipers of male deities such as Apollo or Poseidon were just as tolerant as those of Aphrodite or Ishtar. And like all tales of a vanished Golden Age, the supposed paradise of the goddess disappears upon careful examination. Anthropologist James Frazer notes in his classic, *The Golden Bough*:

> In Cyprus it appears that before marriage all women were formerly obliged by custom to prostitute themselves to strangers at the sanctuary of the goddess, whether she went by the name of Aphrodite, Astarte, or what not. Similar customs prevailed in many parts of Western Asia. Whatever its motive, the practice was clearly regarded, not as an orgy of lust, but as a solemn religious duty performed in the service of that great Mother Goddess of Western Asia whose name varied, while her type remained constant, from place to place. Thus at Babylon every woman, whether rich or poor, had once in her life to submit to the embraces of a stranger at the temple of Mylitta, that is, of Ishtar or Astarte, and to dedicate to the goddess the wages earned by this sanctified harlotry. At Heliopolis or Baalbec in Syria, the custom of the country required that every maiden should prostitute herself to a stranger at the temple of Astarte, and matrons as well as maids testified their devotion to the goddess in the same manner. The emperor Constantine abolished the custom, destroyed the temple, and built a church in its stead.[8]

If this is the feminists' idea of a paradise, then they must approve of women being made sex slaves! As for the goddess's paradise on Crete, those peace-loving "matriarchs" seem to have invented the sport of boxing.[9] Anthropologists do acknowledge a lack of fortifications around the palaces of Crete, which they attribute not to an innately peace-loving disposition, but to the island's formidable navy. The goddess herself was known to brandish a long sword, as well as a double-edged ax. Among the artifacts recovered from the Minoan period are numerous spears, daggers, rapiers, and helmets (some with ear-guards and neck- guards).[10] Clearly, the goddess' Garden of Eden as imagined by feminists today has no more basis in reality than its Judaeo-Christian counterpart.

The fiercely monotheistic religion of Islam was founded in the seventh century by Muhammad who "grew up as an orphan in very miserable circumstances,"[11] a situation of adversity amidst wealth not unlike that of Jesus. It is a scenario almost certain to inculcate a powerful *ressentiment*. Mecca was a wealthy city, already a center of pilgrimages for local gods, at the time of Muhammad's birth there around the year 570. The writings of Muhammad, like those of the founders of Christianity, are filled with "the contempt for worldly possessions, the strong condemnation of the arrogance and frivolity of the unbelievers, the warnings against laughing, joking, and careless speech." Both Jesus and Muhammad seem to have been consumed by a gnawing fear that somebody somewhere might be enjoying life. Today, while Christianity and Judaism have had sufficient time and motivation gradually to undo much of the harm done to their culture by the ferocity of their resentments, Islam has not yet found the opportunity to awaken itself from its own medieval stupor. I remain confident that this will someday happen, although probably not within our lifetimes.

Thus we now understand how the monotheists' One Jealous God originated as a reaction among envious and impoverished peoples outraged by the wealth of the advanced civilizations of the ancient Middle East, in resentment against their achievements. We also see that the real enemy of human progress is not intolerance or fanaticism per se, but rather the rabid envy giving rise to those despicable traits. Using Voltaire's term, the true driving force behind *l'infâme* is not blind belief, but envy—and this should not surprise us, for what other motivation possesses the power to whip human emotions so quickly into such a frenzy? Thus, to battle superstition will do little without also battling envy; indeed, left-leaning humanists work vainly to defeat religious belief while at the same time fanning the very flames of *ressentiment*, heating that belief to white-hot incandescence. Only when the focus of the humanist's approach centers on the harm and the inappropriateness of envious behavior will the secular, rational outlook have any realistic chance to prevail.

NOTES

1. Edward Gibbon, *Decline and Fall of the Roman Empire*, chapter XV (New York: Modern Library), vol. 1, p. 445.

2. Ibid., chapter XV, vol. 1, p. 387.

3. James M. Robinson, ed., *The Nag Hammadi Library in English* (San Francisco: Harper & Row, 1981). Creator-God as malicious envier: "The Testimomy of Truth" (9, 3, 47, 14), p. 412; the good being above envy: "The Tripartite Tractate" (1, 5, 12, 2), p. 92; "The Gospel of Philip" (2, 3, 65, 31), p. 139; "The Teaching of Silvanus" (7, 4, 101, 17), p. 354; envy-engendered death: "The Hypostasis of the Archons" (2, 4, 96, 8), p. 159.

4. *Tertullianus Against Marcion* 2:16.

5. Salo Wittmayer Baron, *A Social and Religious History of the Jews* (New York: Columbia University Press, 1952), pp. 32–33.

6. Nathaniel Weyl, *The Geography of American Achievement* (Washington, D.C.: Scott Townsend, 1989), p. 131.

7. Robert Sheaffer, *Resentment Against Achievement* (Buffalo, N.Y.: Prometheus Books, 1988), p. 23.

8. Sir James George Frazer, *The New Golden Bough* (Williamstown, N.J.: J. G. Phillips, Inc., 1965), section 218, p. 298.

9. "There is evidence that boxing existed by about 1500 B.C. in ancient Crete." The *New Encyclopaedia Britannica* (1984 ed.), s.v. "Boxing." Boxing was a frequent theme in Minoan art.

10. The weapons wielded by the goddess, and those who worshiped her, are described by R. W. Hutchinson in *Prehistoric Crete* (Baltimore, Md.: Penguin Books, 1968), p. 248–56. Some accounts suggest that human sacrifice may even have been practiced in goddess-loving Crete, the inspiration of the legend of the fierce Cretan Minotaur. C. W. Ceram suggests in *Gods, Graves, and Scholars* (New York: Bantam Books, 1972), chapter 8, that the celebrated "bull jumpers" of Crete may actually have been sacrificial victims. For a debunking of claims of ancient matriarchies, see Nicholas Davidson, *The Failure of Feminism* (Buffalo, N.Y.: Prometheus Books, 1988), pp. 182–85.

11. *Shorter Encyclopedia of Islam* (1953 ed.), s.v. "Muhammad."

7

In Hoc Signo Decadence Conquers: Esthetic Objections to Christianity

> " . . . *One does well to put gloves on when reading the New Testament. The proximity of so much uncleanliness almost forces one to do so. . . ."*
> Nietzsche, Der Antichrist 46

Speaking personally, I feel that the most telling objection to be raised against Christianity is the esthetic one: what kind of value system is being promoted here? What things are elevated while others are reduced? How did the new Christian world differ from the pre-Christian in esthetic terms, in matters of science and knowledge, in sanitation, in terms of human dignity? When these questions are allowed, their answers cause the apologist for Christianity serious embarrassment.

THE GREAT UNWASHED?

Certainly the cause of public health cannot be said to have been advanced by the birth of Christianity. Jesus' disciples shocked the Pharisees by eating bread with their hands "defiled," that is, unwashed, a violation of Jewish dietary laws, and of civilized custom and sanitary practices as well (Mark 7:3; Matthew 15:2). Given the dismal level of sanitation prevailing in many places two thousand years ago, eating with unwashed hands would be a greater risk to health than today. But Jesus replied to the Pharisees that he saw nothing wrong in that: "to eat with unwashen hands defileth not a man" (Matthew 15:20). Since the matter of the "unwashed hands" is found in the oldest gospel, it is somewhat more likely to represent historical fact. The influential New Testament scholar Rudolf Bultmann demythologized many of the supposed "sayings" of Jesus, by noting their dependence on preexisting sources. But Bultmann regarded the advocacy of eating with dirty hands as among the few authentic "sayings" of Jesus, principally because it represents "a new disposition of mind."[1]

It is significant that the fastidious Luke, the only Synoptic writer to have mastered elegant Greek, omits Jesus' advocacy of such slovenly practices, which, we must infer, he found offensive. Luke's admonition to his "most excellent Theophilus" in verses 1:1–4 not to trust anyone's account of the life of Jesus but his own shows that he probably intended to put to rest problems such as this. In the *Papyrus Oxyrhynchus 840*, a surviving fragment of an extremely ancient and otherwise unknown gospel, Jesus likewise stands in opposition to "purification" by bathing and washing of feet, delivering a vigorous defense of being unwashed.[2] It would seem that the historical Jesus probably did oppose sanitation and hygiene.

What kind of moral instruction is Jesus offering here? Christians must assume that the almighty Father sent down his Son to tell mankind that if they want to eat their food with filthy hands, it is perfectly all right with him. Surely, in his omniscience, Jesus should have seen the harmful health consequences of violating this law, and should have urged his disciples to follow it scrupulously. After all, "the poor" will all-too-eagerly relapse into slovenly behavior when those who know better cease urging otherwise. Those of us who have been raised on the adage "Cleanliness is next to Godliness" have been misled. We have a right to be at least a little shocked upon learning that the Deity—at least as the early Christians conceived him—stood squarely on the side of filth. One would expect a higher standard of behavior from an omniscient and endlessly benevolent Savior.

JESUS, A COWARDLY BEGGAR?

While Christians extol Jesus' character and manner of living, sometimes even using the example of Jesus' "perfect life" as a rationalization for continuing Christian worship after losing faith in the religion's myths, there is compelling evidence that the reality was quite different. Indeed, the very nature of Jesus' character seems to provide much that is objectionable, especially after recognizing that anything terribly unpleasant has obviously been deleted from the "good news" of the gospels. Celsus charged that Jesus went about "begging so disgracefully, cowering from fear, and wandering up and down in destitution." Even though these charges depict Jesus' life in an exceedingly bad light, *Origen did not challenge this picture of Jesus in any way*, which suggests that these aspects of Jesus' life were common knowledge in the second and third centuries. Instead, Origen replied that "it is not disgraceful carefully to avoid running straight into dangers," when one considers the significance of Jesus' mission.[3]

This view of a furtive Jesus is supported by John 7:1, in which Jesus flees to Galilee to avoid arrest; John 8:59, which depicts him hiding in the Temple from those who would throw stones at him; and by John 10:39, in which Jesus somehow evades those seeking to capture him. It is further supported by a number of Synoptic passages in which Jesus either hides, or instructs those who were supposedly healed by him, or who believe in him, not to tell anyone.[4] Origen does, however, vigorously dispute Celsus' characterization of Jesus as "a pestilent fellow."[5] Of course, the image of a Jesus who goes about hiding, cowering, and begging runs absolutely contrary to centuries of painstakingly constructed Christian myth, which makes much of Jesus' heroic resignation. Yet these ancient pagan-era controveries are far more likely to reflect historical reality than the propaganda handed down after Christianity came into power. I find it inconceivable that a Deity would send down his Only-Begotten Son, or even a prophet, who would behave in such a scurrilous manner. Clearly, Christianity entered the world when people who actually do spend their lives begging, cowering, and wandering about created a God in their own image.

JESUS' OBJECTIONABLE MORAL LEADERSHIP

The Jewish religious authorities obviously did not see in Jesus an example of a "perfect life," but quite the opposite. They viewed him as a deceiver, one who "mocked the words of the wise," leading the people astray into apostasy and idolatry. There is a passage in the Midrash (a rabbinical commentary on the Scriptures) depicting Jesus as one of three great enemies of Judaism (along with Baalam and the Roman emperor Titus), being punished in Hell. Conjured up via sorcery, Jesus describes his punishment: "By boiling filth . . . for a teacher has said, "Everyone who mocks at the words of the wise is punished by boiling filth."[6] Clearly, Jesus was perceived by them not as someone noble, but as one filled with *ressentiment*, who with cocky ignorance mocked the wisdom of the grave and sober.

Judging by what we've seen, it seems that Jesus' legacy to the early Christian saints was one of slovenliness and self-loathing. Our first example is St. Anthony, who was the first to gain great fame through the practice of the ascetic, solitary Christian lifestyle. St. Athanasius, who befriended him and subsequently wrote a *Life of Anthony*, boasts of that saint's holy horror of clean water, which Anthony's feet had never touched since his adoption of the Holy Rule, except where it absolutely could not be avoided, such as when crossing a river.[7] When a value system promotes filth as a virtue, one must view it with maximum suspicion.

Many monastics tormented themselves with heavy crosses and chains, or by fastening their weary limbs to massive iron restraints. To neglect one's hygiene and need for bodily motion until one developed pus-filled open sores was considered a mark of great holiness. One could hardly aspire to become a great ascetic saint or holy man without displaying some such badge of sacred suppuration. The celebrated St. Simeon Stylites pursued holiness by spending many years of his life sitting atop a pillar, high in the air. Not surprisingly, his body gradually became covered with sores, which then were infected with maggots. People came from far and near to see this saintly wonder, and the God of the Christians seems to have approved of these maggots immensely. One day Basilicus, king of the Saracens, picked up one of the maggots that had fallen from Simon's body to the ground, and for some inexplicable reason was seized by the urge to lay it upon his eye. It is reported that this maggot was then instantly transformed into a magnificent pearl, which the king valued immensely.[8]

So strong was the link between holiness and hideousness that many actively sought deformity for Christ's sake. There are numerous accounts of women who prayed to become sufficiently disgusting to escape all dangers of sins of the flesh. Perhaps the best example is provided by St. Angadrema of seventh-century France. Having vowed her virginity to Christ, she was horrified to learn that her father had arranged for her to marry a young nobleman. Wishing neither to break her holy vow nor disobey her father, she prayed to God to be made hideous. Her prayers, it is said, were answered. The night before her marriage, she was struck with a hideous leprosy, and her suitor fled. Even more remarkably, her deformity is said to have left her as soon as she joined a convent, safe from all danger of sex. When St. Angela of Merici was just a child, she often used to wash her beautiful hair with soot and water, to spoil its beauty.[9]

The entire tradition of monastic practices provides much that is objectionable to a civilized person. Viewed from afar, the monastic life seems to be pure and lofty, but examined closely it can inspire little but revulsion. Gibbon, whose eye for hypocrisy and imposture was seldom fooled, was not impressed by the sham of selflessness and piety in those early monastic orders:

> The monasteries were filled by a crowd of obscure and abject plebeians, who gained in the cloister much more than they had sacrificed in the world. Peasants, slaves, and mechanics might escape from poverty and contempt to a safe and honorable profession, whose apparent hardships were mitigated by custom, by popular applause, and by the secret relaxation of discipline. . . . The pusillanimous youth preferred the penance of a monastic, to the dangers of a military, life. The affrighted provincials of every rank, who fled before the barbarians, found shelter and subsistence; whole legions were buried in these religious sanctuaries; and the same cause which relieved the distress of individuals impaired the strength and fortitude of the empire.[10]

Thus Gibbon did not think it mere coincidence that the era that saw the rise of Christian monasticism also saw unprecedented success in barbarian attacks upon the Roman world.

Some orders of early monks sought to mortify the flesh by actually blurring the distinction between humans and animals. Gibbon noted that "the numerous sect of Anachorets derived their name from their humble practice of grazing in the fields of Mesopotamia with the common herd. The great St. Ephrem composed a panegyric on these *boskoi*, or grazing monks."[11] This remarkable passage probably inspired Nietzsche's repeated linkage of "Christians and cows," most notably where Zarathustra proclaims, "Except we be converted and become as cows, we shall in no wise enter the kingdom of heaven."[12] Probably hardly anyone reading Nietzsche realizes that this is not mere satire, but a wry comment on historical fact.

Such actions strike our modern sensibilities as bizarre in the extreme. Yet they are not such a different form of *resssentiment* than is found in the teachings of Rousseau, who found romance in a harmonious-but-imaginary "state of nature"; or of Thoreau, who in *Walden* urged men to live outdoors in a wooden box; or for that matter from the pronouncements of today's radical eco-*ressentiment*, with its battle cry "Back to the Pleistocene!" However, these more recent ascetics, unlike their predecessors, are wont merely to write and talk about the abolition of civilization and/or humanity, without actually putting their words into practice. Even the sainted Thoreau eschewed all *genuine* wilderness, camping out on Emerson's property at Walden Pond, making frequent forays into Concord for supplies, companionship, and reading material. As for his latter-day disciples, the world has yet to see a herd of grazing ecologists.

JESUS, THE SOWER OF DISCORD

Other examples of the teachings of the Jesus of the gospels are equally objectionable. (We know little if anything for certain about what Jesus *actually* said, but of course the authors of the books of the New Testament were the real founders of the Christian religion.) "Suppose ye that I come to give peace on earth? I tell you, Nay; but rather division," proclaims the Prince of Peace in Luke 12:51. "For from henceforth there shall be five in one house divided, three against two, and two against three. The father shall be divided against the son, and the son against the father; the mother against the daughter, and the daughter against the mother; the mother-in-law against her daughter-in-law, and the daughter-in-law against her mother-in-law." A nearly identical threat is made in Matthew 10:34–35.

What Jesus is made to say here is, I think, that he intends to inculcate *ressentiment* between the generations. Friction between Christian and pagan members of the same household became a significant social problem, a development that Churchmen apparently noted with malicious glee. The degree of fanaticism expected of the Christian was such that he or she was supposed to abandon not only property but family ties as well. Father, mother, children, and spouse were to be jettisoned by these fanatics like so much useless encumbrance. No doubt many of those who did not go so far as actually to leave their family began to neglect their family obligations. How fundamentalist conservatives reconcile destructive statements like these with their professed "pro-family" attitudes, I cannot imagine. Nor can I fathom any way for pro-family preachers to rationalize away Luke 14:26: "If any man come to me, and hate not his father, and mother, and wife, and children, and brethren, and sisters, yea, and his own life also, he cannot be my disciple."

Mark 9:40 has Jesus speak the reassuring words, "For he that is not against us is on our part." Because Mark is our earliest gospel, its account of Jesus' life and sayings is probably the least unreliable of the four. Jesus may (or may not) have spoken words like these. But this gentle sentiment was then reversed in Matthew 12:30 and Luke 11:23: "He that is not with me is against me." This reflects a sentiment of fanatical intolerance, one that came to be paraphrased or repeated many times by violent revolutionaries beginning in the 1960s, the decade of flaming *ressentiment*. The gentler passage we saw earlier was eliminated entirely by Matthew, but we see it reflected once again in Luke 9:50: "He that is not against us is for us." The reason for this can only be conjectured. Of course, the Church Triumphant, coming to power long after these gospels were written, answered this question in the harsher manner, condemning to everlasting torment everyone who "is not with us."

CHRISTIANITY: ABSURDITY EMBRACED

Another major objection that the thinking person must raise against Christianity is that religion's explicit rejection of human reason. The human facility for abstract rational thought, the one clear difference between our species and all others, is explicitly rejected by Christianity because it "leads us astray." The Church Father Tertullian dismissed the problem of the absurdity of Christian beliefs with his famous doctrine *credo quia absurdum est*, "I believe it *because* it is absurd."[13] Having reached this point, we might just as well hang up our brains to dry with the wash, and join the herd of monks grazing contentedly in the fields. Nietzsche, with typically keen insight, suggested that the Christian might consider going just one step farther, proclaiming *credo quia absurdus sum*, "I believe it because *I* am absurd."[14]

Indeed, whoever insists on remaining a committed Christian must deal forthrightly with the problem that there are simply *no* intellectually satisfactory proofs for even a single major tenet of the Christian faith.

Perhaps the best argument to be mustered in favor of Christianity is Johann Sebastian Bach's *St. Matthew Passion*. Listening to a really outstanding performance of such a work puts one into a frame of mind conducive to an acceptance of the Christian worldview. But note that it is not precisely an intellectual argument that sways us. Emotion, not logic, lies behind conversion experiences. The music of Bach has undoubtedly won far more converts to Christianity than has the philosophy of Thomas Aquinas.

In one remarkable passage in *The Decline and Fall of the Roman Empire*, Gibbon gives us a hint of his own private views of Christianity's origins, an opinion that many of the other eighteenth-century *philosophes* shared but seldom dared to utter. Here Gibbon uses the trick of stating an extremely impious and shocking position as if it were not his own, and feigning to be offended by it; censorship and blasphemy laws were still powerful forces to reckon with. Gibbon's contemporary, Voltaire, used this same technique with devastating effect: he would set forth some grossly impious argument in loving detail, then pretend to be horrified by it. Reading between the lines, the following harsh assessment of Christianity, attributed to the "malice and infidelity" of "an enemy," would seem to be a view Gibbon himself shared:

> The new sect of Christians was almost entirely composed of the dregs of the populace, of peasants and mechanics, of boys and women, of beggars and slaves, the last of whom might sometimes introduce missionaries into the rich and noble families to which they belonged. These obscure teachers (such was the charge of malice and infidelity) are as mute in public as they are loquacious and dogmatical in private. Whilst they cautiously avoid the dangerous encounter of philosophers, they mingle with the rude and illiterate crowd, and insinuate themselves into those minds whom their age, their sex, or their education has the best disposed to receive the impression of superstitious terrors.[15]

Note how this parallels Nietzsche's charge that the Roman Empire was not actually defeated, "but ruined by cunning, secret, invisible, anemic vampires! Not conquered—only sucked dry!"[16] This, Gibbon hints, was the *real* story behind Christianity's successful conquest of the Roman Empire.

NOTES

1. William Barclay, *Introduction to the First Three Gospels* (Philadelphia: The Westminster Press, 1975), p. 56.

2. In Ron Cameron, *The Other Gospels* (Philadelphia: The Westminster Press, 1982), p. 54.

3. Origen, *Contra Celsum* 1:61.

4. Mark 7:24, 7:36, 8:26, 8:30, 9:9, 9:30; Matthew 8:4; Luke 8:56.

5. Origen, *Contra Celsum* 2:29.

6. R. Joseph Hoffmann, *Jesus Outside the Gospels* (Buffalo, N.Y.: Prometheus Books, 1984), p. 47 [b. Gitt 56b, 57a].

7. Athanasius, *Life of Anthony*, chapter 47, quoted in the editor's note to Gibbon's *Decline and Fall of the Roman Empire* (New York: The Modern Library), vol. 2, p. 349.

8. Theodoret, *Church History* (fifth century); quoted by E. Cobham Brewer, *A Dictionary of Miracles* (Philadelphia: Lippincott, 1884), p. 415.

9. Brewer, *A Dictionary of Miracles*, pp. 388–90.

10. Gibbon, *Decline and Fall of the Roman Empire*, chapter XXXVII (Modern Library ed.), vol. 2, p. 355.

11. Ibid., pp. 361 and 361n.

12. Friedrich Nietzsche, *Zarathustra* IV, "The Voluntary Beggar."

13. Tertullian, *De Carne Christi* 5.

14. Friedrich Nietzsche, *Morgenrote* 417.

15. Gibbon, *Decline and Fall of the Roman Empire*, chapter XV (Modern Library Ed.), vol. 1, p. 440. Celsus makes this same argument; see R. Joseph Hoffmann, ed. and trans., *On The True Doctrine* (New York: Oxford University Press, 1987), pp. 72–75.

16. Friedrich Nietzsche, *Der Antichrist* 59.

8

The Blessed of Christ

" . . . And he lifted up his eyes on his
disciples, and said, Blessed be ye poor; for
yours is the kingdom of God. . . . But woe
unto you that are rich! for ye have received
your consolation. . . ."

Luke 6:20, 24

What has been the ultimate effect of the triumph of Christian belief
and Christian values? Given that Christianity was able to permeate
the very body and fabric of Western society, what have been its
consequences? Surely Nietzsche was given to overstatement when he
wrote in *Der Antichrist*:

The whole labour of the ancient world *in vain*: I have no words to
express my feelings at something so dreadful. . . . Every prerequisite
for an erudite culture, all scientific *methods* were already there . . . the
free view of reality, the cautious hand, patience and seriousness in
the smallest things, the whole *integrity* of knowledge—was already there!
already more than two millennia ago! . . . ruined by cunning, secret,
invisible, anemic vampires! Not conquered—only sucked dry! Covert
revengefulness, petty envy become *master*![1]

Obviously, the entire labor of the ancient world has *not* been in vain; our debt to their accomplishments is incalculable. Nonetheless, Nietzsche's point merits much consideration. It is extremely important to consider how the Western world changed as a consequence of the triumph of Christianity. What causes and what arts have been advanced? What has been hindered? What has been rendered more likely to occur, and what less so? What has come to be valued more highly, and what less? Whose likes and dislikes are embodied within this new scheme of valuation, whose grousing is therein elevated to sanctity? Let us dare to look at the phenomenon of Christianity from the perspective of *cui bono?*: who benefits from that outlook, and who loses?

Obviously, the most direct beneficiaries of the triumph of the Christian outlook are the unproductive, who are now able to exalt their wretchedness as a holy state. Failure to achieve economic self-sufficiency not only ceases to be an embarrassment, but can actually be proclaimed a virtue. Indeed, the presumption of immorality has, thanks to Christianity, passed from the inert to the active, from the wretched to the successful. Whenever a resentment-based system of morality prevails—whether socialist, fascist, or jealous monotheist—that life-enhancing sense of virtue triumphant passes from disciplined achievers to envious failures, from the self-reliant to the unreliable, perhaps even to the wantonly destructive. This is probably the single greatest harm caused by Christianity and other resentment-based religions—the theft of the sense of virtue from the truly virtuous, and its appropriation by those who would use its intoxication not to enhance but to throttle the joy of existence. The very zest of unselfconscious, goal-directed activity, of accomplishment without guilt, has been undermined by Christian values.

Among those who have lost the most from Christianity are surely our independent thinkers, those finest flowers of human intelligence. They have found it necessary to conceal their virtues to avoid offending their neighbors; sometimes, indeed, to preserve their very lives. Describing his era in which enthusiasm waxed for the first flowering of socialism, the poet Yeats wrote, "The best lack all conviction, while the worst are full of passionate intensity."[2] One could not want a better description of an era of *ressentiment*. Clearly, the triumph of Christianity in centuries past had the identical effect. Any doctrine that emboldens the ignorant while demoralizing the capable is pernicious in the extreme. "It is impossible to read the New Testament without feeling a partiality for that which is ill-treated in it," charged

Nietzsche. "Even the Scribes and the Pharisees gain advantage from having such an opponent: they must have been worth something to have been hated in such an indecent fashion."[3]

BENEFITS ATTRIBUTED TO CHRISTIANITY

What are the benefits resulting from the Christian outlook? It would be grossly unfair were we to look only at the problems caused by Christianity without considering its benefits, and it would be absurd to pretend that no advantages have ever been conferred.

The Sanctity of Life

Clearly, an individual human life is now valued more highly than in pagan times. We no longer look with indifference—or even amusement—upon others being put to death, as did many Romans watching a crucifixion, or a death in the arena. This obviously represents an advance in civilization. Moralists have long attributed the concern for the prevention of unnecessary death and suffering to Christianity, and one could not possibly deny that Christian values played a part in its spread. But was Christianity the only factor at work here, or even the principal one? Might other factors have promoted this advance quite independently of Christianity?

Stoic moral philosophy was already a leading force in the intellectual life of ancient Greece and Rome by about 200 B.C. In the popular mind, Stoicism simply means enduring hardship, and the competing Epicurean philosophy is identified with hedonism. While this is not without some truth, the two philosophies have been more accurately characterized in this way: "Because Stoics are more concerned with reducing suffering in human life than with increasing its pleasurable aspects, they propose an ideal which is very different from the one proposed by Epicureans. Yet, both Stoics and Epicureans are concerned with enhancing well-being."[4]

The noted classicist Edith Hamilton wrote: "In an age of cruelty, widespread as it never was to be again, the Stoics declared the cruel man to be possessed by 'a dreadful disease of the mind' which reached 'the extreme of insanity when pleasure was felt in watching a human being die.' . . . The principle which became fundamental in Roman law, that all men are by nature equal, was derived, historians agree, from the Stoics."[5] The ideals of compassion and human equality are almost universally and unquestioningly believed to have their origins in Christianity. Yet to the extent that they represent moral progress, they must be credited primarily to the philosophy of Stoicism, and not to Christianity. Since Stoic moral philosophy was already well established in the Greco-Roman world long before the birth of Jesus, it is much more reasonable to argue that Christianity served as a vehicle for the spread of certain positive Stoic ideals than it is to see these ideals as primarily Christian. Let us also not forget that Christian churches have themselves been among the worst violators of the rule of the "sanctity of human life."

The Work Ethic

The work ethic making possible the prosperity of the productive nations of Western Europe and North America is commonly known as "the Protestant ethic." This is asserted by some to be an indispensable element in building an industrious, prosperous society. Some conservatives are wont to claim that were it not for the Protestantism underlying that ethic (or, in the diluted form of the argument, without "Judeo-Christian values"), modern industrial society could not exist. Sociologist Max Weber gained the attention of the world by setting forth such a claim. At one time Weber's argument may have seemed invincible, when the major Protestant nations dominated the world's commerce; but from today's perspective it can be readily challenged. At present the economic position of predominantly Protestant countries is in a steady relative decline, being overtaken by groups and nations in which Christianity has played little or no role. Looking at data for the United States, Nathaniel Weyl discovered that the eight ethnic groups with the highest "performance coefficients" (with a coefficient of 100 representing the average) in seven "core indexes of contemporary achievement" are: Jews, 488; Indians, 384; Sikhs, 347; Chinese, 271; Koreans, 227; Japanese, 212; Swedes and Welsh, tied at 117.[6] Thus the religious cultures that are the most hospitable to achievement are not only non-Protestant but non-Christian as well: Jews, Hindus, Sikhs, Buddhists, and Shinto. The highest-achieving Protestant groups trail far behind, only marginally above average. To attribute the financial and professional success of Jews, Buddhists, and Hindus to "the Protestant ethic" is worse than absurd. The case for belief in the unique value of "the Protestant ethic" is today about as hopeless as that for "scientific socialism." The best we can say is that while Christianity itself seems to be a major hindrance to achievement, the work ethic of mainstream Protestants is less impaired than that of other Christian sects.

Charity

Charitable acts are so frequently deemed "Christian charity" that it seems to many that the phrase contains a redundancy: the very concepts of "Christianity" and "charity" seem to be intertwined. Yet what is the reality of this? The ideals of generosity and hospitality toward one's guests are extremely ancient; they were customs central to ancient Greek society and hence far predate Christianity. As for charity, Jews were putting this into practice centuries before Christianity even began. Once again, we see that while Christianity picked up some positive ideas, and probably helped them to spread, in no way can Christian thought be credited with the origin of concepts like generosity or charity.

Redistribution of Wealth

Many people think that without Christianity, we should never have had the innovation of granting to the poor "income transfers" from the taxpayer at large. But such social welfare schemes antedate Christianity itself. For example, the Roman "corn laws," a program to provide subsidized food to the poor, were enacted into law as the *frumentariae leges* starting in 123 B.C.[7] Furthermore, the practice had been carried out as a custom for centuries prior to becoming law. Of course, the experience of recent years has caused even many one-time supporters of social welfare schemes to question the wisdom of routinely penalizing the most productive citizens to subsidize the inactivity of the least. But whatever one's opinion of programs of this kind, the fact remains that they existed long before Christianity. There is little in any "Great Society" program that did not exist in pre-Christian Rome.

CHRISTIANITY AND ENVY CONTROL

It would seem, from what we have said already, that whatever benefits we can realistically attribute to Christianity are overwhelmed by a floodtide of harm resulting from the triumph of so much envy, fanaticism, intolerance, and superstition. Hence the triumph of Christianity must be regarded, on the whole, as a tremendous net loss to civilization.

Yet while the above viewpoint, which emphasizes Christianity's negative effects, is accurate historically, perhaps it presents an incomplete picture of the role that that religion plays today. Despite their origins in the resentments of the uneducated against an advanced civilization, monotheistic religions evolved long ago into systems of envy control, a prescription for give-and-take between the envier and the envied. Although the envious, begrudging God now universally worshiped was invented millennia ago as an envy-weapon to destroy the mighty civilization of Babylon or Rome, as each religion came into power, its focus necessarily changed from destroying a civilization to running it. All successful revolutionaries inevitably face this same challenge: suddenly it is in their interest to cease inculcating envy and anger against those who shoulder responsibility, and instill instead perfect obedience and respect.

Thus Christianity, as it exists today, has become a highly developed system of envy control. It is often able to provide a degree of self-control for those who have none of their own. It can sometimes lessen the envious suffering of the undisciplined as they look upon the affluence of the productive, turning what might otherwise become a destructive rage into passive acceptance. If the rules that one must follow are believed to have come directly from God, with the priesthood merely acting as a conduit, then those who are angered by the necessity of following *any* rules can discover no one on earth whose power is to be envied, since all are simply following God's will. Christianity also can often deflate the envious rage that today is very commonly turned by feminists against their husbands, thereby preserving marriages and stabilizing the home environment in which children live. Thus religious people are far more likely to have stable marriages than their nonreligious neighbors. The envious resentment felt by teenagers against their parents is likewise frequently mitigated by religious doctrines that proclaim obedience to parents as the Will of the Lord. The invidious comparisons necessary for generating envious malice do not occur when it is believed that differences between individuals are decreed by God himself.

No one could deny that these can be important advantages for the survival of a society, and it is probably precisely because of these advantages that jealous monotheisms have survived. Even a system of envy control having major harmful side-effects will, in many circumstances, be better than having none at all. Christianity allows the resentful to turn their envious anger toward persons safely *outside* their own group. It may be against "unbelievers" or against "the worldly"; the resentments may even turn against groups that really don't exist, such as "Satanists" or "witches." But unfortunately, it is equally likely to turn against other faiths, perhaps against "the Jews," or against "heretical" Christian sects. While the "jealous God" system of envy control undoubtedly confers some advantages, these very advantages are purchased at a tremendous cost: intolerance, xenophobias, ignorance, and often bitter sectarian hatred. This is why religious societies that demonstrate great social cohesiveness do so at the cost of enormous difficulties in dealing with outsiders. Surely better schemes must be possible to prevent society from being torn apart by the envious *ressentiment* of children against their parents, women against men, and the indigent against the successful.

Hitler offered Germany a system of envy control that was harmful in the extreme, yet highly effective. He told his followers that all their problems were caused by Jews and also by Communists, the Jews' supposed accomplices. Therefore, all of the resentments of the defeated German people were deflected from the privileged Nazi elite, which wonderfully united the country, but at a cost of tens of millions of deaths and a Europe left in ruins. Lenin and Stalin erected a similar system for channeling outward the resentments of the Soviet-dominated people, the same people whose angry resentments had, after all, toppled a mighty ruler just a few years earlier. They were told that all their problems were the fault of capitalists and of the bourgeoisie, and that history itself (a process remarkably similar to "the will of God") had decreed that things must work out exactly as they had. Therefore, it became utterly inappropriate for any degree of envy to be manifested toward the privileged Soviet elite, who, after all, represented the workers, and not some greedy, self-serving individual (whom one *can* compare oneself with and hence envy). As further insurance against being envied, Soviet Marxists proclaimed that the proletarian revolution was "inevitable." When a situation is genuinely believed to be "inevitable," one cannot compare the actual with the possible, since the two must be identical. This effectively defuses all *ressentiment*, which is fueled by an ongoing process of invidious comparisons.

True believers in systems of monarchy are spared any envy of their ruling families, whose reign is perceived as entirely "natural" and proper, and presumably divinely sanctioned. Since the average citizen in a monarchy cannot realistically compare his station with that of a king, or duke, or prince, venomous envy of such an elite does not usually develop. After all, God has decreed one man to be a prince, another to be a peasant, and God's will must be obeyed. Similarly, believers in a religion of One Jealous God are told that the existing system of popes and cardinals (or ministers or rabbis or presbyters or mullahs) is ordained by God, exactly as it stands. Therefore, should any envious anger be directed at such a hierarchy, it would be an affront to God himself! Since one cannot compare oneself to those whose privileges are decreed by God, powerful resentments against church hierarchies do not usually develop, so long as the religion is unquestioningly believed.

SYSTEMS OF ENVY CONTROL: SOME FINAL THOUGHTS

What all such systems of envy control have in common is the message: "Your low station is a consequence of God's will (or of our enemy's perfidy); it is not appropriate to envy the existing hierarchy, whose rule is entirely just and exists for your benefit, not their own." Compare that message with its opposite, the resentment-mongering of the rabble rouser who does *not* hold power: "Your low station is the result of the villany of your society's elite!" The former is trying to preserve a society by diverting resentments outward (where they may, as a side effect, cause great harm to others); the latter seeks to destroy a society by fanning the flames of resentment within it.

The envy weapon is a high-caliber engine of destruction and, like a cannon used for crowd control, it is certain to claim large numbers of innocent victims. Where envy already exists in abundance, it must be defused: perhaps those who are already envious must be made religious! At least their destructive passions might then be channeled onto less harmful paths. Yet it is clearly a mistake to attempt to purchase social harmony by fanning powerful resentments against outsiders, since this requires the continual stirring up of ever-increasing doses of *ressentiment*. The total quantity of envy created in this manner is generally greater than the amount dissipated, resulting in a net disadvantage.

Far better than the generation of powerful torrents of envious venom that must then be imperfectly deflected is the promotion of social patterns in which envy is perceived as inappropriate. For centuries philosophers have warned of the danger and harm of envious behavior. Indeed, this seems to be perhaps the *only* thing that virtually all major philosophers of the past have been able to agree upon. They cannot agree about whether God exists, or whether the will is free, or even if the world around us is real. Yet virtually every major philosopher, writer, and thinker of the past has agreed that envious behavior is extremely widespread, and extremely harmful. Among those stating this view quite directly are Pindar, Herodotus, Democritus, Aesop, Antisthenes, Aristophanes, Socrates, Aeschylus, Plato, Aristotle, Cicero, Horace, Ovid, Seneca, Plutarch, Augustine, Aquinas, Bacon, Milton, Shakespeare, Dryden, Spinoza, Hume, Smith, Kant, Holbach, Schopenhauer, Melville, Kierkegaard, and Nietzsche.[8] As the nineteenth century passed into the twentieth, the awareness of envy dimmed. Today's social scientists must be infinitely wiser than those thinkers named above, for their writings record their belief—as Schoeck clearly demonstrates—that no significant human behavior is motivated by resentment or envy.

It would probably be in society's interest to have the level of awareness of envy extremely high, and for envy to be perceived as something shameful, an emotion utterly unfit for a civilized person. Psychotherapist Joseph Berke observed that "not all societies are like ancient Greece or Renaissance Italy, where envy was accepted as a fact of life."[9] Perhaps what allowed the above-named eras of greatness to soar above merely ordinary times was a keen awareness among the finest achievers of the envious malice being ceaselessly directed at them from below. Thinkers have often wondered what might be done to bring back the glories of the days of Socrates, or of Leonardo. Perhaps one key element is: educated people must be keenly aware of envy, must recognize its every manifestation, and must hurl back every envious comment as a reproach to whoever uttered it. In our own time, people have been sensitized to recognize utterances betraying racism and anti-Semitism, and to reject such thinking totally. Perhaps we can reach the point where manifestations of envy and resentment elicit a similar response.

At the same time we must be careful not to be excessively hard on those religionists who are themselves victims as much as victimizers. While self-defense against their harmful doctrines is a legitimate action, vindictiveness is not. These people were in virtually every instance assaulted early in their lives by a jealous monotheism, with no opportunity for escape. They did not consciously choose to become envious, but rather had the decision practically forced upon them by the insidious behavior of those around them. I cannot see these people as deserving of any punishment whatsoever. At the same time, the venom they carry must not be spread.

Today I surprise myself with my evolving position of grudging respect for the ability of moderate Christian sects to function effectively as systems of envy control, doing no great harm either to the Christian or to those whom he must deal with. After all, the typical Methodist, or Roman Catholic, or Episcopalian for the most part goes through life in an entirely rational and secular manner. They do not act very differently from their nonreligious brethren. They do not go off and fight Crusades, or battle the heathen, and the Inquisition has been inactive these past few centuries. Their religion costs them a little time and a little money, but the cost is bearable, and in return it may offer some very tangible advantages. Their family life is likely to be far more stable and far less troubled by the strife of envious resentment than that of their nonreligious fellow citizens. Because they are more likely to stay married, they will probably enjoy higher living standards than those who lose expensive houses in divorces and pay substantial sums for child support, lawyers, and alimony. Because their children are more likely to accept the idea of adult guidance and supervision, they are less likely to be led by their own *ressentiment* into self-destructive behavior patterns. In the wealthiest neighborhoods of the major American cities today, one finds that close to 100 percent of the children come from families that are active church members. The percentage in less affluent areas is far lower. One can convincingly argue that these families have arrived into such expensive surroundings, and have managed to stay there, *because* they have their own potentially destructive resentments securely under control. It is reasonable to suspect that their religion plays a large part in that. However, I am greatly troubled over the fact that religious-based systems of envy control require one to *tell lies.* Such a system will gradually but inevitably be eroded, however, as our increasing knowledge of the universe undermines the foundations of ancient myth. Morality cannot long survive as a house divided, when social harmony is in opposition to truth.

Perhaps we can now identify that elusive reason for the failure of secular humanism to establish itself as a viable life-stance for the millions: humanism offers absolutely nothing in the way of envy control. In fact, by its frequent alliance with socialist and feminist *ressentiment,* humanism sometimes actually fans the flames of envy, thereby placing strains on the personal lives of those who embrace it. Humanism surely does not lack morality, as its critics have charged. Humanism does not result in the breakdown of civilized restraints, or in the abolition of truthfulness, or generosity, or charity. All those positive traits humanism possesses in abundance. But for those who are inclined toward envious feelings and behavior, humanism as it now stands offers absolutely nothing to discourage invidious comparisons. In fact, it tends to encourage them. It likewise offers no protection to the envied. For this reason, humanism as a social doctrine will likely always remain of marginal significance, limited primarily to the childless, to rootless cosmopolitans, to angry, highly educated but low-income radicals—in short, to those who have no reason to fear being envied.

Envy is the "stuff" with which jealous monotheisms operate. It is the clay with which they sculpt; the fabric they weave; the water in which they swim; the commodity they buy, sell, and trade. Since Roman times, virtually the entire Western world has called upon one "Jesus Christ" whenever it has needed to deal with matters of envy. If you fear the envy of your less affluent neighbor, religion offers you protection by telling him that God has commanded him not to covet your goods. In return, God orders you to hide your intelligence, power, and/or success behind a veil of modesty and humility, in order not to antagonize the other's wrath. If you are troubled by your envy of someone whose wealth and power are not dissimulated by humility, religion comforts you by promising that the wealthy person will be punished by unending torment. Should any society somehow succeed in reducing envy to negligible levels, the supposed "need for religion" would disappear.

No doubt it is the recognition of the need for envy control—even if they do not know the term—that convinces conservatives of the absolute necessity of religious belief for social cohesion. They have an excellent issue here, but do not know how to express it directly. Indeed, one might perhaps define a conservative as "someone who worries about the need for envy control." Unfortunately, in their eagerness to deal with this problem, conservatives will all too often grab onto whatever existing system of envy control may be in place, no matter how outdated, narrow-minded, or destructive, and attempt to enforce its prescriptions with a Procrustean vengeance.

Perhaps the fundamental issue behind *ressentiment*, more fundamental still than "resentment against achievement," is the question of "assertion vs. submission": how does one decide when to assert one's own will in one's dealings with others, and when to defer to theirs, or to rules applying equally to all? The criminal element of any society will opt for "assertion at all times, and at any cost." We frequently encounter this in the underclass in large cities: the absolute insistence on self-assertion and the immediate gratification of every whim, no matter who gets hurt, and no matter what the long-term consequences. One whose outlook is dominated by *ressentiment* is utterly incapable of submissive behavior, even when it is in his own self-interest, even when impartial justice requires it. Christianity's answer to that question, and the answer of the true conservatives, is precisely the opposite: submission in all things. "Resist not evil, for my kingdom is not of this world." That answer is, of course, just as unworkable as the other.

The thoughtful person will surely see that there is not, and can never be, any infallible guide telling us when to assert our will against others, and when to submit. We must instead be content with the inexact but helpful guidelines we get from philosophy, from history and psychology, from the arts, and, yes, sometimes even from religious teachings. We submit to the authority of others when it is in our own self-interest, and when the protection of everyone's rights requires it. We assert our own wishes, feelings, and desires when we think it proper to do so, and when no great harm seems to follow therefrom. We are submissive to teachers and employers, to our benefit. We likewise submit to the law, so that everyone may be protected. Yet we realize that even these guidelines are not foolproof; often even trusted persons, and persons in authority, will take advantage of us should we become habitually meek. Thus neither the immediate assertion of every whim, on which the "liberated" resentful insist, nor the suppression of every desire, the church-triumphant's avowed aim, makes for a workable guide.

There is a sense in which one's tendency toward self-assertion is related to one's level of self-esteem: the more "worthy" one feels, the less will one be willing to submit one's will to general rules. This suggests that the currently fashionable efforts among educators unconditionally to raise students' "self-esteem," quite apart from any real accomplishments on their part, may actually be counterproductive. It squelches any inclination that low-achievement students might otherwise have for self-improvement. Many people *already* possess levels of self-esteem that, considering their circumstances, are unjustifiably high. Adolph Hitler and Charles Manson, for example, obviously possessed levels of self-esteem that were as extreme as they were unjustified, with tragic results. The world cannot be blamed for wishing that they had acquired, somewhere along the way, some trace of self-doubt. There are many who have good reason for doubting themselves, and they should not always be dissuaded. The optimal situation for society would be when, to paraphrase Yeats, "the best are full of passionate intensity, while the worst lack all conviction." Such apparently was the case in pre-Christian Greece and Rome.

Some might question the legitimacy of the very notion of envy control, viewing it as a tool for "exploitation" or "oppression." But without at least some means of controlling envy, a society cannot long endure. If anything has been learned from the global failure of socialism, it is that a society cannot be viable unless its productive people are permitted to keep and enjoy the fruits of their own labor. But whenever and wherever the productive live better than the unproductive, some members of the latter group will simmer in envious anger. Unless there exists some mechanism to counteract that anger, some force tending to minimize their envy and hold it in check, the anger of the envious will eventually explode with murderous force. When this happens, all incentives to produce are destroyed, and the society's future likewise perishes.

But even after recognizing the need for a system of envy control, it is unwise to embrace the first such scheme one encounters, especially one that relies heavily on false and absurd claims. A society's reliance for its envy control on a doctrine as shaky as Christianity makes it perpetually hostile to truth, fearing to allow discussion and inquiry to proceed freely lest the fragile pillars of social concord come crashing down. The battle between religious teaching and scientific knowledge, between biblical texts and critical thought, will never end. When we permit our envy control to be dependent upon doctrines at odds with the truth, should we tilt too far in the direction of unhindered inquiry, we risk the growth of malicious envy that we will be unable to control. Yet should we err instead in the direction of piety, we risk loss of our personal freedoms, and imperil our economic prospects as well. How vastly better our prospects for lasting social harmony if our system of envy control, and objective fact, were not at odds, if promoting reason and controlling envy were mutually supportive, not in opposition. A society capable of creating that kind of system of envy control will prevail as has no other.

We must keep in mind that stability for its own sake is not our supreme goal. An isolated tribal society in the bush might be stable over thousands of years. But such societies typically control envy by the ruthless suppression of individual differences as well as by prohibiting all innovation. The innovator is, after all, the figure despised by the envious more than any other. Every innovator proclaims, "I know better than *all* of you!" Therefore, one society after another has stumbled upon the simplest (and cruelest) method of envy control: prohibit all innovation. Liberty and envy are everywhere locked in mortal combat. As the liberty of a society increases, the opportunity for envy increases tremendously. Invidious comparisons multiply as people take advantage of their freedom to live differently, to act and dress differently, to make more money, or to enjoy more leisure time. And as a society reins in individual differences to lessen envy's pangs, liberty must necessarily suffer.

Has a "rational" system of envy control ever existed? The question is intriguing. The ancient Athenians had a crude, but effective, way of dealing with those who were intensely envied. Anyone might, for any reason, be exiled by a vote of the citizens. That way, anyone whose wealth, fame, or overall good fortune seemed too much to be endured could at any time be driven from the community for a number of years. Certainly the constant fear of being exiled made the wealthy and the powerful tread very carefully, avoiding doing anything that would unnecessarily antagonize ordinary citizens. They often made grand gestures to win popular approval.

The Romans apparently hit upon a formula that yielded stability for approximately a thousand years, yet still allowed them to become the most powerful and the most sophisticated civilization on the face of the earth. They envisioned their many gods as benefactors and protectors of the Roman people, and imagined their prosperity to derive from them. Therefore, it was both wrong and futile to envy the wealthy, since the gods had decreed it. (Calvinists resurrected a similar form of envy control, and before long became the most prosperous people in Europe.) The fusion of gods and state, of emperor and god, and the trivial sacrifice continually made to these gods, freed the Romans from the dangers that they feared atheism might bring. The common people sacrificed to the gods because they believed it would bring divine favor, while the educated, who knew that the gods of Olympus were just poetic fictions, went through the same motions nonetheless as a gesture of respect to the emperor, the senate, and the people of Rome. Observe how the Christian (as well as the Jewish) religions appear to have been custom-crafted to undermine a society that viewed its emperor as a deity—as emperors are still viewed in Japan—and required little rituals to thank its tutelary gods a dozen or more times every day.

For a system of envy control to be effective, it must of course be widely and wholeheartedly believed. Is it possible to devise an effective system of this kind without telling lies? The level of overtly envious behavior in present-day Japan is exceedingly low. The Japanese seem to have developed a highly effective system of envy control based on an ethic of mutual cooperation and respect. Religion does not play a large role in the lives of the Japanese people, thereby demonstrating that secular envy control is indeed possible. Nietzsche believed that a democratic state would not long endure because it lacked the kind of *mysterium* that a state grounded in a monarchy or in traditional religious myth possesses.[10] Not long after I read that passage, and while I was still reflecting on it, I watched on television as President Reagan, joined by President Mittérand of France, unveiled the newly restored Statue of Liberty. This made for excellent theater. Clearly Nietzsche had been wrong, I reflected, in saying that a democratic state could have no potent *mysterium*, no "transcendent institution." If what I was watching was not a powerfully captivating political *mysterium*, then I cannot imagine what would be.

I do not have all the answers for fashioning an effective system of envy control not grounded in religion, but clearly the robe of the Statue of Liberty is the kind of fabric from which one might be woven. Indeed, such a system already *has* in part been fashioned, but is not recognized for what it is. After all, there is far less envy of wealth in the United States than in most other countries. But let us not become complacent about what we have. Rare is the system that cannot be improved! The free democratic states possess, indeed, a tremendous advantage over resentment-based ideologies, because to be *for* an icon like the Statue of Liberty does not require one to be *against* any other group. It does not represent *ressentiment* directed at someone else's success, nor does it begrudge happiness to others. The same cannot be said of zealous nationalists, racists, or worshipers of a jealous God. Such people are indeed united, but unfortunately by a powerful common hatred. Perhaps we have here a litmus test of whether a particular system of envy control is dangerous or benign: is there any nationality, race, or religion that it requires one to be *against*?

The political and ideological world consists of many value systems in endless contention. Every doctrine or ideology is, at bottom, the expression of *somebody's* desires and interests. As such, none of them are "true" in any cosmic sense: not Christianity, not socialism, not democracy, not feminism, not libertarianism, or any other doctrine. For each, ask *cui bono?* And none of them are absolutely "false," either, so long as they represent somebody's value system. This does *not* mean, however, that the adoption of any particular value system is a matter of indifference, since some ideologies promote tolerance and understanding, while others fill peoples' minds with hatred and envy. What we should ask in evaluating each is: What would be the consequences if this value system increased its power, and had the opportunity to realize its professed ideal? What is the value of this value?

There is no one system of values that, if made universal, would satisfy everyone. Even the most beneficent and tolerant of ideologies would leave at least some people suffering in a stew of envious malice at the sight of others' success. Political problems will not all be solved on some glorious future day when "the libertarians" or "the humanists" or "the people" come to power; individuals will inevitably abuse whatever social institutions exist, seeking their own advantage. Hence pluralism, and the contention that it brings, is required not merely in practice, but in theory as well. No Utopia is possible: the productive will not be happy if they cannot retain the fruit of their labors, while the indigent will remain unhappy so long as the productive are left unplundered. Therefore there is no scheme that both groups would perceive as totally fair.

It would be wrong for any ideology, even for the best of them, to seek a final victory, a permanent exclusion of all others. For every human desire becomes a philosophy, striving to generate an ideology under which it can justify its own fulfillment, with all objections rationalized away, appropriately or not. The role of ideology, when freely adopted, is to permit one to do what one wishes to do, anyway. Even when a value system is firmly grounded in universal rights and justice, there will always be zealots seeking to intrusively expand it into the inevitable gray areas where legitimate interests collide. For most people, morality seldom extends beyond self-interest. No matter which ideology may be recognized under law, *all* ideologies will exist in fact, even if only in secret, since conscience and emotion cannot be legislated. Pluralism is always a fact in every society, even in those situations where heterodox views must hide. As soon as the reins of repression in the Soviet Union began to loosen, dozens of ideologies and factions sprang up as if from nowhere. All those factions must have existed in previous years, but were obliged to speak in whispers.

There is no conceivable law to be passed that will prohibit invidious comparisons. Envy will always be with us under any political system, in any conceivable Utopia. Therefore let us train ourselves to recognize its every manifestation, learn to call it by its proper name, and battle it for the hearts and minds of people. Let us strive not for some foolish Utopian goal of scoring a final victory over envious ideologies, but rather devise the best possible means for keeping them in check, for promoting achievement in the face of resentment. That is the real challenge facing those of us who seek to promote a tolerant, humane, pluralistic worldview: devising a value system that will provide the kind of envy control that only religion has heretofore provided, *without* the injurious side effects that a jealous monotheism invariably entails.

NOTES

1. Friedrich Nietzsche, *Der Antichrist* 59, trans. R. J. Hollingdale (Baltimore, Md.: Penguin Books, 1968).

2. W. B. Yeats, *The Second Coming.*

3. Friedrich Nietzsche, *Der Antichrist* 46.

4. Ben Kimpel, *Stoic Moral Philosophies: Their Counsel for Today* (New York: Philosophical Library, 1985), p. 33.

5. Edith Hamilton, *The Roman Way* (New York: W. W. Norton & Co., Inc., 1932), chapter 7.

6. Nathaniel Weyl, *The Geography of American Achievement* (Washington, D.C.: Scott-Townsend, 1989), p. 21. The seven "core indexes" of achievement are inclusion in: 1. *Who's Who in America,* 2. *American Men and Women of Science,* 3. *Frontier Science and Technology,* 4. *Poor's Directory of Directors,* 5. *Who's Who in Finance and Industry,* 6. *Directory of Medical Specialists,* and 7. *Who's Who in American Law.*

7. *Harper's Dictionary of Classical Literature and Antiquities* (1965 ed.), s.v. "Frumentariae leges."

8. Most of these passages (and many more) can be found in Gonzalo F. de la Mora's *Egalitarian Envy: The Political Foundation of Social Justice* (New York: Paragon House, 1987), pp. 3–59, or in Helmut Schoeck's *Envy: A Theory of Social Behavior* (New York: Harcourt, Brace, & World, 1970), chapters 9–11.

9. Joseph H. Berke, *The Tyranny of Malice* (New York: Summit Books, 1988), p. 63.

10. Friedrich Nietzsche, *Human, All Too Human* 472.

Index

187